Fear*less*

Fear*less*

THE 7 PRINCIPLES OF
PEACE OF MIND

Brenda Shoshanna, PhD

STERLING ETHOS
An imprint of Sterling Publishing Co., Inc.

New York / London
www.sterlingpublishing.com

STERLING and the distinctive Sterling logo are registered trademarks of
Sterling Publishing Co., Inc.

Library of Congress Cataloging-in-Publication Data
Shoshanna, Brenda.
  Fearless : the 7 principles of peace of mind / Brenda Shoshanna.
    p. cm.
  Includes bibliographical references and index.
  ISBN 978-1-4027-7067-8 (hc-trade cloth) 1. Peace of mind. 2. Fear. I. Title.
  BF637.P3S517 2010
  152.4'6--dc22

                                          2010003448

10 9 8 7 6 5 4 3 2 1

Published by Sterling Publishing Co., Inc.
387 Park Avenue South, New York, NY 10016
© 2010 by Brenda Shoshanna Lukeman
Distributed in Canada by Sterling Publishing
$^{c}/o$ Canadian Manda Group, 165 Dufferin Street,
Toronto, Ontario, Canada M6K 3H6

Book design and layout: Rachel Maloney

Manufactured in the United States of America
All rights reserved

Sterling ISBN 978-1-4027-7067-8

For information about custom editions, special sales, premium and
corporate purchases, please contact Sterling Special Sales
Department at 800-805-5489 or specialsales@sterlingpublishing.com.

This book is dedicated to Noah Lukeman, my wonderful agent,
whose unending efforts on my behalf have given birth to this work.

Special Thanks

I WISH TO OFFER SPECIAL THANKS FOR THE LOVE, support, wisdom, guidance, and encouragement that contributed to the writing of this book.

First, thanks to my dear family, who never fail to offer love and support—Danny, Gerry, Melissa, Abram, Joshua, Yana, Adam, Zoe, Remy, Jake, Maya, Zachary, and Cassie.

I want to thank my wonderful editor, Jennifer Williams, whose diligent work and lovely disposition have greatly contributed to this project.

I particularly thank those whose unending friendship, practice, and wisdom have guided me along, including Eido Roshi, Robert Kennedy, S. J. Roshi, Ernie Castaldo, Larry Crane, Michael J. Creeley, Burt Dubin, Haskel Fleishaker, Rabbi Joseph Gelberman, Ed Glassing, Martin Hara, Lindsay Harrison, Gene Krackhel, Richard Schiffman, William Solomon, Bernard Starr, Fay Tabakman, Scott Young, and Ralph Zeitlin.

Contents

Preface

Whoever can see through all fear will always be safe.
—Tao Te Ching

Today, we are a nation bathed in fear. Just a few years ago, it seemed as though opportunities were endless. By and large, jobs were secure, banks were stable, and we could count on the ever-expanding growth of our economy to help us fund our children's future and our own. There was a sense of stability, prosperity, and hope. Most importantly, we felt invulnerable to foreign attack, and confident that our borders would never be violated.

The shocking events of September 11 ushered in a new era, however. Not only were we awakened harshly to terrifying and tragic events, but the sense of being shielded in our own land had suddenly been ripped away. Since then, fear has become a part of our daily lives. Every day, in the months that followed 9/11, we checked to see if there was a red or yellow terror alert. Would the terrorists strike again? How safe would we be that day?

Next came the Iraq war, causing further upheaval, fear, loss, and dissension. The national and international turbulence goes on and on. Today, many of our basic anchors—so much that we once counted on to keep us secure—have been taken away. The world seems to be turning upside down. This is a time of crisis.

However, the Chinese ideogram for crisis means opportunity. When our sense of security is taken away, when we don't know where to turn next—this is a time filled with surprising possibilities for extraordinary growth, discovery, and even fulfillment. Now we are being forced to re-evaluate our lives. The vital questions in front of us are, "What can I really count on? Where does my true security lie? How do I start over? What do I *really* need in order to live a fulfilling life?" These questions are fundamental, the ingredients of a meaningful life. When things go well, we may overlook them. During a time of crisis, however, we are forced to grapple with them every day.

It is therefore of the utmost importance that we stop for a moment and gain clarity and power over fear. If we listen to the false messages that fear brings us, it is easy to become overwhelmed. In fact, the real danger we are faced with today is not loss of income, home, or safety. Our real enemy—the number one terrorist—is the fear we carry within.

We must understand what fear truly is, why it arises, and how we can become stronger than fear and release it from our lives. As we do this, as fear weakens, we can begin to see our situation from the largest perspective possible and get in touch with our enormous inner resources that allow us to handle whatever comes along. We can tap into our fundamental courage, creativity, and wisdom and let them be our guides.

What Is Fear?

It has been said that there are only two emotions: love and fear. For some, paradoxically, love is frightening, while fear feels safe. Many of us depend on fear, thinking it protects us. It can feel good to hold on to fear. At the same time, we are taught that it can be dangerous to be trusting; that love can make us weak. This is the work of fear, creating confusion. Fear thrives on lies. It weakens the immune system, destroys our basic sense of confidence and well-being, takes us off track, and makes us prey to those who wish to control or attack us in various ways. Self-hatred is fueled by fear. Paranoia, an extreme form of fear, can infect every aspect of our being, undermining the very core of our relationships and wiping away the curiosity, playfulness, joy, and love of life that we are born with.

When and Why Fear Arises

When fear takes over, most of us have no way to resolve it, no tools or techniques with which to handle it. Panic attacks, compulsions, obsessions, and other forms of dysfunctional behavior can occur automatically. Fear also arises in love relationships—when we feel vulnerable or, conversely, when things are going very well. Some of us feel as if we do not deserve happiness or intimacy and fear losing the love we have found. Some of us fear illness, death, or just being who we are. The lives we live may feel inauthentic, and we suffer the consequences in many ways. In fact, the reason why such staggering numbers of people in the world are involved with alcohol, antidepressants, other drugs, and all kinds of self-destructive behavior can be directly attributed to the effects of fear.

It takes practice to unravel fear. It is one thing to have an intellectual understanding of what is harmful; it is something else to know how to actually get rid of fear in your life. This book will show you how. Contrary to popular belief, it is not at all difficult to do! It simply takes a willingness to take new steps and see with new eyes. The truth is that fear is a bully: When you turn around and face it head-on, it becomes powerless. As you do so, you see that the very thing that once seemed so terrifying is simply made of dust and dreams.

The Power of Love

Along with exploring the principles of fear in this book, you will simultaneously explore its antidote: the nature and power of love. Most of us are confused about what love really is. It is easy to mistake infatuation, attachment, and dependency for love. In this book, you will learn how to differentiate between real and counterfeit love. In fact, the exercises that dissolve fear simultaneously allow love to arise. And the practice of love simultaneously dispels fear. They are two sides of the same coin.

As you explore the nature of love, you will become familiar with deeds of love and learn how to do (rather than feel) love. You will receive guidelines and unique exercises that promote a healing, fearless response to life, no matter what is going on.

Combining the teachings of East and West, these pages will provide psychological, spiritual, and practical guidance for activating your vast inner resources in dealing effectively with challenges of all kinds. You will be shown how to unlock your inner treasure-house and live from your original strengths, courage, and goodwill.

Each chapter in part 1 explores one of the seven principles of peace of mind and teaches you how to dissolve a related form of fear, transforming it into a source of courage and strength. Along with discussion and anecdotes, the book contains uniquely designed exercises that are simple, enjoyable, and powerful. You will find them within the chapters and also in the form of a workshop in part 3. As you begin to practice these exercises regularly, they will become a natural part of your daily life, and you will see your fears weaken and gradually depart.

It is important to do the exercises in this book every day, even if only for a little while, in order to break harmful patterns. These exercises and processes have been specially designed after years of study, trial, and research. The techniques are intended to restore your inner freedom and your natural wisdom, courage, and creativity. As you do the exercises, you will regain what was originally yours: an innate sense of safety, well-being, and trust in yourself, in others, and in life itself.

Each chapter will conclude with a universal truth that dispels fear and awakens courage. This statement can be taken as a practice. Remember it, meditate upon it, live with it during your daily life. When something happens that causes distress, dwell upon the universal truth and apply it to your situation. Let the truth about the situation replace the fear you feel. These truths are powerful statements that point to timeless wisdom known through the ages. They replace dire warnings, and are inoculations against catastrophic expectations generated by fear. It is important to test them in your daily life. You are not being asked to believe anything blindly, but to explore and find out for yourself.

Among the many tools and techniques included here are: releasing, the power of choice, intuitive knowing, transforming pain into power, dialoguing with inner voices, undoing the control of others, letting go of the need to control, developing focus, centering, mindfulness, and how to develop a grateful mind.

As you embark on this journey, be curious, willing, and open minded, so that you can taste the results for yourself. It takes courage to open the door, bring in light, and see how easy it is to remove the darkness of fear from your life. It takes courage to journey to a new country, but the time comes when you can no longer remain in the place where you've been dwelling or live under a cloud of fear. At this point, the heart rebels, the mind opens, and you remember the place within that is fearless. Then everything becomes possible. Each day becomes an exciting adventure. The whole world turns around.

PART 1

THE 7 PRINCIPLES OF

PEACE OF MIND

Meeting Fear Face-to-Face

ONE DAY AN EARTHQUAKE SHOOK an entire Zen temple. The ground beneath it began to shake, the building collapsed, and the monks were terrified. As the world seemed to be falling apart, the Zen master calmly led everyone to the kitchen, the strongest part of the temple.

When the earthquake subsided, the master said, "Now you have had the opportunity to see how a Zen man behaves in a crisis. I did not panic. I was aware of what was happening and what to do. Taking you to the kitchen was a good decision, as we have all survived without any injuries.

"However, despite my composure, I did feel a bit tense, which you may have noticed from the fact that I drank a large glass of water, something I never ordinarily do."

One of the monks smiled, but didn't say anything.

"Why are you smiling?" the teacher asked.

"That wasn't water," the monk replied, "it was a large glass of soy sauce."

No matter who we are, when an earthquake hits, we all feel fear. It comes upon us in different ways, affecting our bodies, minds, and hearts. It can be experienced as an emotion, an increased heartbeat, sweating, chills, fast breathing, or a sense of dread and impending doom. Then there are the times when, like the Zen master, we are not even aware of our fear and begin acting oddly, unable to tell the difference between a glass of water and a glass of soy sauce.

Being stung by fear is like being stung by a serpent: It fills you with poison, immobilizes your senses, and blocks your understanding of how to act. Therefore, recognizing and releasing fear is a practice that needs to be done daily. The more you do it, the easier it becomes and the less threatened you feel. Once you dissolve fear, you will discover that clarity and spontaneous knowledge of what to do arise. This actually helps prevent many negative events that might otherwise unfold. If a fearful situation has already appeared, you can reduce the toll it takes and calm down by knowing how to dissolve the fear you are feeling, rather than acting on the basis of it. On the other hand, when you allow fear to grow, you may be blowing up what is really a small situation—or even drawing it to yourself. If you constantly dwell on negativity, it's as if you are inviting it into your life. To begin the process of dissolving fear, it's essential to become familiar with its many guises, to see the ways it appears, the effects it has, and how it camouflages itself and infiltrates all aspects of your life.

The Many Faces of Fear

Fear is a trickster that manifests in all kinds of ways: as obsession, confusion, loss of control, or dysfunction in any area of your life. It can be triggered by anything—ideas, beliefs, memories, tastes, smells, and even unconscious thoughts. For example, you might unexpectedly see someone who reminds you of a cruel person from your childhood, and suddenly you become flooded with fear. Or maybe you go into a meeting feeling great and then pick up on the contagious fear of others that quickly dispels your happy mood and leaves you pessimistic, nervous, and glum.

There are other ways, too, that fear creeps up. Another person can threaten you, either consciously or unconsciously. You may sense, for example, that someone is perceiving you negatively and respond to their seeming dislike with fear. At other times, dire messages assault you—you hear that your job is in danger, a loved one is ill, or your partner is flirting with someone else. Any of these dire messages that you give credence to can bring forth an attack of fear.

I say *attack,* because what is terrible about the message you hear is the fear it generates.

REALIZE that if you don't believe the message or the messenger, fear will not appear. It is not the news you hear but the way you react to it—the fear you feel—that immobilizes.

Some people give us negative messages simply to control through fear. When you are in the grip of fear, you can be easily manipulated and controlled, no longer in charge of your mind or spirit. Sometimes fearmongers do this consciously. Other times not. But no matter what situation confronts you, there is an alternative to a life driven by fear: the process of becoming fearless, which can restore your peace of mind.

STOP: Whenever a message is fraught with fear, reject it immediately. Even if you think it might be true, reject it because you do not have the full use of your faculties when you are in the grip of fear. Wait until the fear has vanished to decide if it is true. When you reject the message, your fear will subside and your thoughts will become clearer. There is plenty of time later on to determine if the message is true. (Most of the time it isn't.)

Fear thrives on your belief in it. It needs you to believe the stories, ideas, beliefs, catastrophic expectations, assorted hallucinations, and hypnotic suggestions that it's feeding you. It needs you to see everything it says as true, as dangerous and life threatening. Once you believe the fear, it turns your mind and your heart into putty and causes paralysis.

INSTEAD OF BELIEVING IN THE POWER OF FEAR,
WHY NOT BELIEVE IN THE POWER OF TRUTH?

Before you can see the truth of a situation and reclaim your inner freedom and the full measure of who you are, you have to look fear in the eye. You must be willing to stand back and make its acquaintance. As you do so, you grow to understand fear's machinations, how it arises, what fuels it, and how it disguises itself and takes hold in so many areas of your life. Certain truths about fear can then become clear.

Fear Is a Bully

This cannot be said too often. It is a new mantra that you must adopt and allow to become part of your flesh and bones. The more you attribute power, strength, and reality to fear, the more it takes over your life. No matter how fast you run from fear, it chases you. Fear preys upon those who allow it and who run away from it in all kinds of ways. There are many ways to try to escape—through relationships, drugs, drink, or addictions of all kinds—but no matter which way you choose, fear will always catch up with you. And though you may be conditioned to run from what you feel is dangerous, you are not a puppet controlled by your conditioning—you can stop.

Ralph could not stop working. He brought work home every night, worked all weekend long, and was the first one to arrive back at the office on Monday. His total absorption with work kept him from facing the loneliness and fear he felt in other areas of his life. It gave him an excuse to be by himself and not have to face the demands of intimate relationships or to enjoy any of the other pleasures he craved.

For so many of us, a particular area of life is dominated by an escape from fear. But rather than mindlessly obeying fear's warnings and directions, you can take a new course. You can stop in your tracks and realize that you are just up against a bully, and a stupid one at that.

STOP for a moment and see fear as a bully. See yourself running away from it. Now take a moment to stop running and to turn around. That's all you need do at this moment. Just stop and turn around. A bully takes its strength from your flight and from your fear and anguish. Just by not escaping, not running away, you are stopping fear in its tracks and taking away its steam. Why is it so hard to stand still?

Henry Miller once said, "The only real miracle is standing still." He knew what he was talking about. Fear makes you nervous and restless, creating the illusion that if you keep moving, stay busy, and do something, anything, you will feel better. But any action you take that is fueled by fear is usually destructive and useless. It may be extremely difficult to stop running, stand still, hold your ground, and open your eyes, but as soon as you do, things can change very quickly.

> Master Bukko Kokushi introduced Zen from China to Japan during the Mongol invasions.
> One of his students, Lord Tokimune, said to him, "Master, fear is the worst enemy of my life. How can I free myself from it?"
> Master Bukko replied, "Cut it off at its source."
> Lord Tokimune asked, "Where does it come from?"
> "It comes from Tokimune himself," replied the master.
> "Above all, I hate fear the most," declared Tokimune. "How can I possibly be the source of it?"
> The master replied, "Find out. Find out."

STAND STILL and see where fear comes from. See yourself unwilling to flee from the fear you are feeling. Let it know you refuse to run. What happens to the fear as you do so?

Stepping back, turning around, looking the bully in the eye is all that is needed for the bully to get nervous and start to back down. It knows it's being uncovered for the unreal weakling it is. As you do this exercise, not only are you learning how to reclaim your power, you're beginning to uncover, remember, and live from the core of who you are.

Abandon poisonous food wherever it comes to you.

—*Tibetan Lojong saying*

Most of us are unconscious victims of fear, living under its spell unknowingly, not dreaming of what our lives could really be. We seldom touch the enormous power we all have to be free, brave, strong, creative, happy, loving—to live our dreams and share them with others—to live a life that is fulfilled. But fear refuses us fulfillment; it enjoys our misery.

As you will see in the following chapters, many of us are attached to our misery, feeling that it keeps us safe and secure. As you fight your suffering, you may also be clinging to it, refusing to let it go. What you do not realize is that clinging to suffering is not your true wish. It is simply an effect of fear. The more you become aware of fear's manipulations, the more you will see the ways in which it infiltrates your life, and the easier it will be to let it go.

Fear Stops Us Cold

Sheila had wonderful plans for how her life would be. She sat at home visualizing her beautiful future. She made lists, planned, and imagined how happy she would be when it all came to pass. When asked why she took no action, she always said the time wasn't right. She wasn't ready, the stars weren't in alignment, she would know when the moment came.

Sheila didn't realize that every moment is a good moment. There is no better time than now to begin. Another way fear trips us up is by telling us we can do it later, that we have all the time in the world. We don't. We don't even know if tomorrow will come. Now is the time. Now is a great medicine for undoing fear.

This one moment—Now—is the only thing you can never escape from, the one constant factor in your life. No matter what happens, no matter how much your life changes, one thing is certain; it's always Now. Since there is no escape from Now, why not welcome it, become friendly with it?

—Eckhart Tolle

DO IT NOW. There is always some action you can take, however small, from which you will learn and grow more confident. Find something you can do, and do it now. See what needs to be done in the moment; take a tiny, doable step toward a larger goal. When you do what has to be done now, fear doesn't have the time or space to grow strong. Fear grows in empty spaces, while you are waiting, imagining, hoping, and planning.

Fear Is a Liar

Fear is the great deceiver. When you buy in to the lies it sells, it takes your time, hope, and life force from you. In exchange for the false sense of well-being fear offers, you give away your birthright. In the Bible, Esau sold his birthright for a bowl of lentils. Esau, the firstborn twin, was to be the heir and successor to his father and to the sacred traditions of his family. However, he preferred a happy and carefree life as a hunter and man of the fields. One day, he returned from a hunting trip exhausted and faint. His brother Jacob, feeling that Esau was unsuited to be the heir, proposed to buy the birthright from him, offering a bowl of lentils in return. Famished, and caring about little but his hunger, Esau willingly agreed.

Esau sold his birthright for a bowl of lentils; you sell your birthright for less than that. Fear takes away your true safety, goodwill, happiness, and natural power to thrive, handle difficulties, and be fulfilled. When you listen to fear's lies, obey its promptings and warnings, you've been sold a bill of goods, turned in the wrong direction, robbed of time, energy, and good sense. Why would you allow this? Esau was starving for that bowl of lentils; he couldn't bear the hunger he felt. You are also starving to feel safe and good. While you're ensconced in fear, however, it's impossible to realize what's truly good and where your real safety lies. But there is a secret beneath all this.

TRUTH WIPES OUT FEAR ON THE SPOT.

Just a little light washes lots of darkness away. Even a moment of truth begins to loosen the grip of fear. All the pain, damage, and illness created by fear seem very real, but they can be dissolved easily. As soon as you see the *truth* of the matter, fear loses its power to harm you. As soon as you stand in the truth, cling to it relentlessly, the healing power of love appears. This is a fact. It is an indisputable law of the mind and heart.

THINK of a lie fear told you that you believed and clung to mercilessly. Just realize now that it was a lie. Take a few moments and realize it more deeply. When you realize it's a lie, what happens to the fear?

Now think of another lie. Do the same with that.

Fear Means Nothing

Shana was constantly dwelling on the reasons she was so afraid. She took all her fears about traveling as a sign that she should stay home. Whenever an image of danger arose about a trip, she thought about canceling. First she stopped flying—too many planes were crashing these days. Then she stopped taking trains—you never knew what could happen, she thought. **This fear I feel means something; the pictures I see of trouble and harm are warnings of what is to come.**

However, none of Shana's fearful imaginings meant anything at all. They were all just illusions. The planes and trains arrived safely while she was locked up in her room.

A tremendous antidote to fear is to realize that it doesn't mean anything. It doesn't mean you're going to get hurt, you've done something wrong, or you're on the wrong track. It's a ghost rattling a saber at you. It warns you of things that are not taking place, stirs catastrophic expectations, and even hides true danger. In fact, fear is just a feeling, based upon old thoughts, ideas, beliefs, and expectations you've been taught over and over and are trained to believe. These old thoughts and beliefs become your conditioning, which arises automatically, like heartburn when you've eaten something you can't digest. If there is real danger, you will be in a much better position to recognize it—separate the false threat from the true—after you let go of the feeling of fear.

Fear Is Only a Feeling

Andrew, a good-looking guy in his mid-twenties, stopped going out on dates because he hated the fear that would hit when things didn't go well. As soon as his date became bored or restless, he was sure the next step was rejection. No matter what she did after that moment, it didn't make a difference. Andrew shut down and finally decided it was easier being alone. In fact, he was the one doing the rejecting, although he didn't realize it.

"The only thing we have to fear is fear itself," as the famous quote by FDR goes. There's a sense that fear is dangerous, that it will capsize our lives and efforts. As soon as we feel a little fear, we clench up, shut down, expect the worst to happen, and often lose touch with what's truly going on.

It was the evening of the third day of retreat. We had been sitting in meditation for many hours a day. By now the pain was almost unbearable, and I was exhausted as well. I wanted to go home, my legs were aching, and my back was stiff. I became frightened as time for the evening sitting approached. Three more hours to go. I didn't think I could make it.

I sat down on my cushion and the bells rang out. After the bells, absolute silence. Soon the pain began to mount—and with the pain, fear came as well. There was no way I could escape it. The more I fought it, the worse it became. Not knowing what to do, beside myself, I broke out sobbing. I knew I was disturbing the others, but I couldn't help it right then. The more I cried, the worse I felt.

Then, to my horror, the head student shouted at me loudly, "Shut up or get out. Go sit by yourself down at the lake. Face your fear. Become stronger than it."

At that moment, stunned, I stopped struggling, turned my attention around, and directly faced the turmoil within. The pain and fear went. I went. Instead there was incredible joy.

At that moment I recognized that fear is only a feeling, a wave of energy, a gust of wind that comes and goes, if I let it. I saw that I was not the fear I was feeling. I was the host—not the guest.

Host or Guest?

In Zen practice, and also in the traditional Japanese tea ceremony, a distinction is made between the host and the guest. It is very important to learn how to be a host and how to be a guest. Each role is different. The host creates an environment in which to receive the guest. He welcomes the guest, is gracious and hospitable. The guest arrives, partakes of whatever the host provides, enjoys, appreciates, offers thanks, and departs. The host does not behave like a guest, nor does the guest behave like a host. If that happened, the whole world would turn upside down.

You are the host; fear is the guest. It's important not to switch roles. When you do, your whole world turns upside down. The guest, fear, comes and goes, while you, the host, remain sitting calmly and secure, watching the passing show.

Here are some exercises to help you think of fear as a visitor who is just passing through.

- **WATCH THE FEAR ARISE AND FEEL IT.**
Where exactly does it come from? Where does it go? Where do you feel the fear in your body? Does it become larger or smaller? Can you just let it go? Do you want to?

- **LISTEN TO THE FEAR.**
It may be saying things to you. Do not take what it says seriously. Remember, this is simply the voice of fear speaking. You can thank it for sharing, and then let it go. Sometimes the feeling of fear just wants to be recognized, felt, or heard. After that, it leaves easily. When you thank it for sharing, all its steam goes away.

- **DO NOT ALLOW THE FEAR TO STOP YOUR ACTIVITIES.**
If you have something to say, say it, despite the way you feel. If you have something to do, do it. Before you say or do it, picture the fear evaporating. Breathe it out, send it blessings, and wave it on its way.

In all of these exercises, you are not running from your fear, you are not repressing or suppressing it, but neither are you allowing it to attach itself to you. You are engaging with it in a different way. By thanking the fear for appearing, you realize that you are not the fear. It is simply a feeling you are experiencing. You are always stronger than the feeling. Put the world back right-side up—become the host, not the guest.

The Real Question

Each time fear comes, underneath all its bluster, the question it is truly asking is, "Can you see me for what I am? Will you learn to grow strong as a result of our encounter? Will you tap into the endless resources you have, see through me, stand up to me, or will you fold?" In a strange way, fear can be your friend, if you know how to engage it wisely. How many of us really hear the unspoken questions fear asks? Do you even realize that you are buckling or shutting down in one way or another when fear has taken hold?

Try one or all of the exercises above. Or create your own. Remember, fear is simply a transient energy; it is your resistance to it, your belief in it, that makes it important. When you see fear as nothing much, it drifts away.

The more you do these exercises, the more you become planted in the truth of who you are. As you grow stronger, fear weakens. After a while, you'll find that it hardly arises anymore; or it just surfaces dimly and then departs.

Living Life in an Orientation of Fear

Fear is not only a feeling—it can become an orientation toward life. An orientation of fear is one of restriction, repression, oppression, punishment, guilt, bad faith, and continual vigilance against being hurt. This can make life a living hell.

Mary saved money for years, hiding it in shoe boxes under her bed. She did not trust the bank, her family, her friends, or herself. She spent very little on herself and always looked haggard. When it came time to give gifts, she didn't. Instead, she'd send a card. Everyone assumed she was impoverished. She always commented on how expensive everything was and that you just never knew when something would happen that would take everything you had away.

When Mary died and her fortune was discovered, her entire family was in shock. They said they had no idea she was a rich woman. But in truth, she wasn't. No matter how much she accumulated in those shoe boxes, Mary led an impoverished life. All of her days were spent in an orientation of fear.

If you live in an orientation of fear, little things upset you. Even during happy times, you are always looking for trouble on the horizon. You may be afraid of being blamed, attacked, or humiliated, or you may spend your days blaming others, or life, God, or destiny for the rotten hand you've been dealt.

Maybe you live in bad faith and see no reason to behave responsibly or to trust anyone. You, yourself, cannot be trusted. Nothing means anything. Ultimately, all is for naught. You feel robbed, deprived, and always on the bottom rung of the ladder. Even in the midst of nourishment and plenty, you are unable to see, taste, or enjoy. But it is not other people who are robbing you; it's your own fear. This fear robs you of clarity, kindness, satisfaction, and plenty. It takes these right out from under your nose.

One of the most dangerous aspects of this orientation is that it leads to living a life that is incredibly rigid: You demand that everything should proceed as it has in the past, or according to your personal expectations and demands. You become afraid to let go of anything, and cling to beliefs, customs, rules, schedules, and injunctions that may or may not suit your needs today. And you begin to demand that others live that way as well, or else you reject and condemn them. Not only does living this way arise from fear, but it generates fear every day as well. In this state of being, you are constantly swimming against a riptide.

A TREE THAT IS NOT FLEXIBLE, THAT CANNOT SWAY
IN THE WIND, CRACKS AND BREAKS.

Catastrophic Expectations

> As long as life is a form of dread, it cannot be anything but pain.

Catastrophic expectations arise regularly from an orientation of fear. A catastrophic expectation is the belief or expectation that something awful is going to happen. Sometimes a small difficulty arises and in your mind you immediately blow it up into the beginning of something terrible. For example, you may have a persistent pain in your body and begin to imagine that it is cancer. Then you begin to wonder how advanced the cancer is. Now that this fearful thought has taken root, the catastrophic expectation grows; soon you become convinced that no treatment will be helpful now. It may be time to write your will.

When you finally discover that the pain is only a sprained muscle, the news may even come as a letdown. For some, it's easy to find a distorted pleasure in dwelling upon catastrophe, a falsely heightened sense of being alive, because of all the attention you get or the excitement you feel wrestling with danger.

When catastrophic expectations are activated, even if the event hasn't actually taken place (and most likely never will), you may have a full-blown panic attack thinking about the possibilities. Unfortunately, these possibilities dictate your choices and actions. All kinds of relationships can shut down in your life. The more you hold on to negative expectations, the more you believe in them, and the worse the fear becomes. It prevents you from thinking clearly and hinders your ability to find creative solutions, in the event that the catastrophe you're expecting (or something like it) actually takes place.

Undoing Catastrophic Expectations

WHEN A CATASTROPHIC EXPECTATION ARISES—when you catch yourself worrying about something that could happen or building up something that has happened—stop and get a piece of paper. Draw a vertical line in the middle. On the top of one column write, what is actually happening. On the top of the other column write, what could happen.

In the column that lists what is actually happening, be very careful to write down specific facts. For example, "I have a pain in my shoulder. I've had it for one day." In the other column, make a list of all that could happen, including positive outcomes: For example, "I could have a serious obstruction, or it could be a slight sprain and clear up immediately." As you actually, consciously dream up different expectations, it will become clear to you that these expectations are merely your fantasies—not the truth. Each time you write down another expectation, go back and check the facts. Ask yourself: *What is actually happening right now? Can I focus upon what's actually happening and not what I'm imagining?* When you want to dwell on what could happen, choose to dwell on positive possibilities. Realize that the choice is yours. Write a few more positive possible expectations now, and dwell on those.

Most of all, realize that it is not the actual event that is causing most of the fear you are feeling, but the expectations and fantasies you are dreaming up about it. In this very moment, you can handle whatever is going on. This very moment you are safe, this very moment holds endless possibilities, and this very moment can be filled with joy.

Suffering from a migraine, Neil Young's vision went blurry and he thought both would pass. But when symptoms persisted the next day, the rock star suspected something more. He was shaving and saw something in his eye that looked like a piece of broken glass. It kept getting bigger and bigger and he knew he had to see the doctor right away. After consulting five specialists, by the next morning the verdict was in: Young had had a brain aneurysm, one that required prompt attention. This was Thursday; surgery was scheduled for Monday.

Some individuals might have holed up in self-pity. Young chose to go to Nashville that very night to work on his album. The words and music came fast, some songs in less than fifteen minutes. In this state of hypersensitivity and facing his own mortality, everything he saw inspired him. A phone message from a friend prompted the song "Falling Off the Face of the Earth." By the time he flew back to New York for surgery on March 28, 2005, Young had penned and recorded eight numbers in just four days.

The result of this whirlwind of activity in the face of a life-threatening situation was the album *Prairie Wind* (2005). The songs of reminiscence and mortality struck a nerve, generating positive reviews all over the landscape, not to mention sales; it debuted at No. 1. Young's health? He made a full recovery after the procedure.

—From Extraordinary Comebacks, *John A. Sarkett*

Young put forth a vibration of courage and strength that aided and uplifted him, as opposed to choosing the vibration of fear, which might have destroyed him.

The Vibration of Fear

Fear has a vibration that attracts certain people, events, and situations to it. When you are afraid of dogs, a dog will sense it, bark, and attack. When you feel loving toward the animal, the dog will sense it as well and respond in kind. There is a visceral awareness of the vibration a person emits.

Masters in the martial arts, feeling extremely secure in their ability to defend themselves, can walk down the street in a dangerous neighborhood, and their vibrations of strength and courage deter would-be attackers. Intuitively, unconsciously, viscerally, others sense their strength. There are also stories of famous Hindu *rishis* (masters) who could send out such a total and unambivalent vibration of love that wild animals would come to them and lick their hands.

Our nation and the nations of the world are living in fear of terrorists, failing economies, and threats of attack. The more fear is permitted to run haywire, the worse these conditions become. As soon as we stop, take back our power, begin to dismantle the fear, we will be able to get in touch with our innate peace of mind, our resourcefulness, and the endless solutions that are waiting to be found. There are simple solutions waiting for us, surprising solutions, ways of turning enemies into friends. However, we cannot find these solutions when our lives are based on fear. It is of the utmost importance that we realize the urgency of the situation and firmly resolve to let go of fear and live our lives on a new basis. It is not hard to do either—it just takes willingness.

A New Vibration: The Practice of Love

The truth is that love is so much stronger than fear. Even a little drop of love can dissolve and heal so much fear and pain. Our hearts are filled with this love; we could not survive without it. And yet we are so stingy; we refuse to open our hearts and give. This stinginess, this constriction, is the effect of fear operating in our lives. Therefore, as we learn to dissolve fear, we simultaneously come into the healing presence of love. The practice of dissolving fear is also the practice of love. And learning the practice of love simultaneously dissolves the fear that we feel. Both of these are the most practical, urgent, and enjoyable activities it is possible to undertake.

STOP: Think of a time when, unexpectedly, love burst through in your life. This could be love of a child, an animal, a sunset, a moment of seeing the beauty around you. It could be a time when you received a surprising kindness, overlooked an insult, or suddenly decided to extend yourself to another person. It could be a moment when you forgot your own self-interest and reached for something larger. Dwell upon this. Then dwell upon it some more.

Moments of love are happening continuously, but you do not stop and notice them. You do not take account of them. Take them in. Relish their effects on you. You are so preoccupied by fear that these moments of love might even seem unimportant. They are not. They take place regularly and deserve your attention.

WHATEVER YOU PAY ATTENTION TO IN YOUR LIFE
INCREASES AND INTENSIFIES.

What do you want to pay attention to—love or fear? What do you want more of in your life? This is an important question. You always can choose where to focus your attention.

PAY ATTENTION to a moment of love, and then pay attention to another. Take note of the effect it has on you. Take note of the effect it has on others as well.

TURNING POINT

Taste and See That Life Is Good

The Bible says, "Taste and see that life is good." This statement stands up to fear and laughs in its face. It is a refutation of fear. It is a statement of truth. For those who live in fear, life does not taste good. But when fear dissolves, the sweetness and nourishment of life are restored.

When someone gives you a dire message, when your catastrophic expectations start to grow, immediately replace them with this statement of truth. Say to yourself, *Taste and see that life is good.* Focus on that. Dwell on it deeply. When the fear has passed, you can look at whatever piece of news you were given with calmer, clearer, and wiser eyes. And if there is something that needs to be done, your innate knowingness will reveal it to you.

ONE

PRINCIPLE 1

The Courage to Be Who You Are

The ways we think we are, rather than the ways we truly are, are the bars on our personal prison.
—ZEN SAYING

MARTIN BUBER, AUTHOR AND BIBLICAL SCHOLAR, spent many hours at his university studying, writing papers, and receiving guests. He also received students and others who sought his counsel. Buber would allocate a certain amount of time to them, listen to their questions and problems, and offer a response.

One day a student came to him and asked for guidance. As usual, Martin Buber listened to his problem, or so he thought, and then he responded as best he could. The student thanked him and left the office. Buber went back to his books. All was in order, or so he thought. It was not until the next day that Buber discovered that after the meeting, the young man had gone back to his room and hanged himself.

This stunned Martin Buber. He could not think, speak, or open a book. For days, he simply dwelled upon the student and pondered this question: What is it that a person truly needs when he is desperate and goes to someone for help?

After many weeks of pondering, Buber found his answer. He decided that when a person is desperate and goes to another for help, what he truly needs is a "presence" through which he knows that nevertheless, despite anguish, there is still meaning.

From that time forward, Buber closed his books, let go of his religious practices, and disregarded his name and title—all of which, he felt, had kept him from being fully present for others. Instead, he simply focused on becoming completely present and available to all of life. He focused on living from his authentic self. By discarding all the trappings and distractions, he kept himself focused on the truth of the moment. He allowed himself to have the direct experience of others and was able to respond to them from his deepest truth. When visitors came to him, they found someone at home.

The Inauthentic Self

When you spend your life presenting a false front to others, it's easy to lose touch with your deepest reality—your authentic self. It becomes difficult to hear what others are truly saying or what they need from you. Your words become routine and empty; people listen and are not moved. It is only when you put aside your false self that true presence and love arise. This is the healing we all want, which brings unshakable peace of mind.

Throughout most of our lives, we play a variation on the game of Let's Pretend. We say, "Let's pretend that you didn't say that and I didn't hear it. Let's pretend that what happened really doesn't matter. I'll help you keep your pretenses up, and you help me keep up mine." From the time we are young, we are taught to create a public personality to please others and hide much that is real. Little by little, however, this false personality, or ego, takes over, and we live in constant fear of being found out—discovered to be someone other than who we seem.

Pretense robs our true life from us. If someone knocks on your door to visit, more often than not there's no one home. It can be quite scary to live in a world where it's hard to find someone to really listen, respond, and care. And of course, there is nothing more healing, and no better antidote to fear and loneliness, than to find someone who is truly "there." In those moments, you become "at home" with yourself as well.

A student visited a wise teacher, desperate to know how to live.

"What do you seek?" the wise teacher asked.

"Enlightenment—peace of mind," replied the harried student.

"Why do you search outside? You have your own treasure-house."

"Where is my treasure-house?" gasped the student.

The teacher replied, "What you are asking is your treasure-house."

The student's eyes were suddenly opened.

After that, he often urged his friends, "Open your own treasure-house and use those treasures."

—*Zen story*

Usually we do not open our own treasure-house; instead we spend most of our time and energy acquiring skills, knowledge, and strategies—anything to build up our false self. Unfortunately, no matter how much time and attention we devote to this, it never brings real joy or peace.

No matter how much praise the ego receives, it never feels really approved of or loved. By its very nature, the ego is skittish, fearful, and ungrounded. It constantly craves more and more approval and regularly feels threatened. The ego cannot distinguish between what is useless and what is valuable. It eats too much, makes wrong choices, and refuses to face reality. Living on this basis, we live in fear.

The Three Poisons

According to the Buddha, we are all born in the grip of three poisons: greed, anger, and delusion. These poisons are afflictions, and some of us have more of one than another. They are the fuel for the ego, causing it to be defensive, suspicious, and manipulative and to camouflage itself in all kinds of ways. Yet no matter how much powder, paint, jewels, and new clothes the ego wears, no matter how many times it hears "I love you," it basically feels ugly, and hates itself and everyone else.

Even though Amy's boyfriend told her he loved her over and over again, she didn't believe him. She needed to hear it again and again. "Why do you love me?" she kept asking. Of course this became exhausting for her boyfriend, who, feeling drained, ultimately left.

Why do we cling to our disturbing egos? Because we have no idea how magnificent we truly are.

Leaving the Garden of Eden

How does a false self start to grow and gain power over us? We are born full of joy, curiosity, and the desire to grow into who we uniquely are. Each child comes into life with her own particular songs to sing, lessons to learn, challenges to face. She is able to live each moment fully, calling out for food when she's hungry, reaching for love when she feels alone. She responds to her own inner needs and callings and interacts with the world in her own particular way.

Before the demands of others take hold, before family, social, and religious conditioning kick in, the little child has an intrinsic sense of who she is, what she can give to others, and what she needs to receive. She is a child of life, a member of the universe. There is a sense of belonging, safety, and trust that all that is needed will be provided. This is a condition of optimum well-being.

As the child grows and interacts with others, the sense she has of being at home in a safe and supportive universe fades. The world often begins to stand in opposition to her desires and can seem filled with danger. She must struggle and fight for what is hers, has to suddenly cover up and hide. Anxiety and dread arise. Before long, the child begins to feel that there is something fundamentally wrong with her—that she is not lovable and doesn't belong. The poison of the serpent has taken hold.

As the child leaves the natural self of childhood, she creates a self to please others and earn the love and approval that was originally hers. Now she is further exiled from her basic wholeness and wisdom. This split haunts many of us. Living cut off from our natural selves, we no longer have a true foundation to stand on. The whole world becomes unreal and unsafe.

Exiled from Our Natural Selves

> *In social moments we see how estranged we are from each other.*
>
> —*Paul Tillich*

Not aware that we have rejected ourselves, we live with the constant fear of rejection by others. This fear is particularly vivid in relationships and in the workplace, where there is tremendous pressure to look good, fit in, and fulfill endless demands. In order to do so, we find ourselves living more and more from the false self. Unknowingly, we have accepted the guidance of fear.

Of course, sooner or later this backfires. The resentment and despair of living as a false self is too much to bear. No one can tolerate it continually. You need the basic strength and resourcefulness that come from living from and accepting the truth of who you are. Living from the false self ultimately causes panic attacks, rebellious behavior, illness, anger, and other forms of protest. No matter what hardships come into your life, no matter what turn events take, if you have yourself, you also have the natural ability to handle whatever comes along. There are tremendous gifts and inner resources available when you have the courage to be who you are.

A certain Sufi was asked, "Why does that dervish [teacher] over there make so many mistakes?"

He answered, "If he made no mistakes, he would be either worshipped or ignored. He makes mistakes so that people shall ask why he does what he does."

"But what is the advantage of that?"

"The advantage is that people may see that which is behind him and not the man himself as they imagine him to be."

—*Indries Shah*

Looking for a True Man or Woman

Why do we feel so compelled to wear masks, play games, and delude ourselves and others?

There is a story about Diogenes, a philosopher in Greece, who went around town with a lit candle, looking for a true human being. Most likely he had a hard time finding one. Even in times of old, the longing to find a true person, and the difficulty of doing so, was clear. This is a fundamental example of the power fear holds in our lives, the web of lies it weaves. The pressure to conform is very great. Many people believe there is something wrong with them because they are different. They establish their value by comparing themselves to everyone else. But as you look at yourself through the eyes of others, you become an object to yourself and a stranger.

Seeing Yourself Through the Eyes of Others

Maria never felt satisfied. Whatever her husband bought her was not up to par. It didn't compare to the gifts her friends received from their husbands. Her gifts weren't wrapped as well, were less expensive, and seemed to be last-minute choices. Her friends' husbands spent considerable time, money, and attention choosing their gifts, and the women received gifts more often. Little by little, this took a toll. It caused friction not only between Maria and her husband, but also between Maria and her friends. Instead of representing love to her, her husband's gifts began to diminish her sense of self-worth. She saw them as evidence that he didn't really care, and that she wasn't worth much in his eyes.

Maria was entirely in the grip of her false self, perched on an identity that had to fall apart. She knew her value only by comparing herself to others. She needed gifts and other outward signs of attention to affirm her identity. Her entire identity was externally based, dependent upon the behavior and responses of others. The fact that her husband loved her dearly, and that she was a worthwhile and beautiful woman, was completely lost to her. What had started as a fulfilling marriage began to fall apart.

Living from the False Self

What you tell me about me,
Tells me more about myself
Than what I know about me
From within.

—Jean-Paul Sartre

When you live from a false self, you give more credence to the responses of others than to what you feel and can learn by yourself. You accept the thoughts of others as true and doubt your own feelings and responses. In this manner, you lose contact with what is authentic and meaningful and become an easy target for fear. How long can you live the reality of others? Can you ever gain enough approval in someone else's eyes?

We are not leaning willows—we can and must detach ourselves.
With the exercise of self trust, new powers appear.

—*Ralph Waldo Emerson*

Fear warns us to conform to the reality of others, or else we will be shamed and thrown away. Of course, the opposite is true. The more you extricate yourself from the reality of others, connecting with and living from who you really are, the stronger, more vivid, and more worthwhile your life becomes, and the less you live in the grip of fear.

STOP A MOMENT and notice where you feel most able to experience who you truly are. Where are you most fully accepted? When and where do you feel able to accept others fully as well?

Developing Self-Trust

I must be myself. I cannot break myself any longer
for you. I will so trust that what is deep is holy
that I will do whatever inwardly rejoices me and
the heart appoints.

—*Ralph Waldo Emerson*

From deep within all of us there is a longing to be real, to express and know ourselves fully. When you are able to take off your masks, not only can you breathe, but your life then becomes renewed. But taking off your masks may not be so easy. You may have become so accustomed to wearing your masks that you confuse them with your own skin. Although your masks may constrict at every turn, you fight to the death to keep them on.

Another lie fear tells is that masks constitute your security and beauty; what's underneath is scary and ugly. Of course, this just isn't so. Some people would rather die than have their masks taken off. They cling to the masks they wear the way a drowning man clings to a lifeboat. If the mask is insulted, they respond with fear and anger. Others would kill to uphold their public image. Some kill themselves when their image is gone. Even when they're quite ill, some people are still primarily concerned about how they look to others and the impression they make. They live behind the fortress of their masks until the very end. But the changes we encounter in life eventually wipe out all images and take our masks and games away.

NOTICE what kind of mask you are wearing. Draw a picture of it. Complete the following sentences:

I want others to see me as . . .

Underneath my mask, I am . . .

Look at your responses carefully. What is this mask truly doing for you?

We create masks to meet the masks of others. Then we wonder why we cannot love and why we feel so alone. But remember, everything the mask says and does is for the purpose of hiding. Can one mask love another? Does a mask know how to communicate? How much of your mask are you willing to relinquish? How much fresh air will you let into your life? Do you realize what the mask is keeping out? Could it be that although you long for it, love is your deepest fear?

Where Has the Love Gone?

The false self becomes especially active in love relationships. For many couples, the first months of a relationship are glorious, as they live out and project their fantasies upon each other. Each becomes someone different, having left huge parts of themselves unexpressed. Naturally, this can only last so long. Usually after six to nine months, other aspects of the couple's nature begin to be revealed. This is the point when so many say, "I don't know where the love went." Or, "I love you, but I'm no longer in love."

Of course, it is not the love that went anywhere; it is the false, fantasy self that is beginning to crack apart. The false self cannot remain indefinitely, and when other parts of our personality begin to emerge, what is thought of as love seems to disappear. Usually, we spend most of our time trying to make someone into a person who meets our dreams or needs. When they can't or won't change in the way we want them to, we complain that we don't know where the love went. In fact there was no love in the first place, only need and manipulation.

Charles was devastated. He idolized his mentor, the person who was everything he longed to be. After about a year of studying with him, Charles found out secrets about his mentor's life that shocked him totally. They were in direct opposition to everything the mentor taught and seemed to be. Charles couldn't eat or sleep and was stricken to the core.

"How could he betray me like this?" Charles said over and over. "He's ruined everything. I feel like a fool for having loved him so much. Whatever he taught was garbage. I'll never trust again."

A friend of Charles listened. "You didn't love the teacher," he said. "You loved your image of him, your fantasy about who you wanted him to be. When you know the truth and still love him, then you're doing something. Otherwise, don't call it love! That's the real lesson he's teaching you."

When you build a life based upon an image of who you have to be or who another person has to be in order to be valued, you are building your life on sand. You are not really able to know or love the person, only your fantasies. At any moment things can change, other parts of this person can be exposed, and your dreams can be pulled out from under you.

There is a beautiful story describing a Zen master and his nephew. This story presents a different way of being with others. It points to where love truly is, and what is needed for a person and a relationship to truly grow.

A Zen master's brother called him one day and begged him for help with his son. This boy, the Zen master's nephew, was unruly and getting worse. No matter what the brother tried to do, the young man wouldn't listen. He was out late at night carousing, drinking, listening to wild music; he wouldn't obey his family at all. The master's brother was desperate. "We are at our wit's end. I need you to come to our home for a week to help."

The Zen master agreed. He went to his brother's home, unpacked, and greeted his wild nephew warmly. The nephew didn't know what to expect. The Zen master then simply decided to spend the week accompanying the young man wherever he went. He went along with the nephew to the bars at night, joined his group of friends. The young man waited to hear a scolding when they came home, but the Zen master said nothing at all. He then accompanied his nephew to parties, rock concerts, houses of ill repute, wherever the young man went. At the end of each day the young man waited for a lecture, but it never came. The Zen master simply joined him, kept him company wherever he went.

Finally, the week ended, and the young man didn't know what to think. The time came for the Zen master to go home, and he went to his room to pack his things. Sad that his uncle was leaving, the young man joined him. He sat quietly watching his uncle pack. Still no words of guidance were offered. Then the Zen master bent down to tie his shoelace, and as he did, a tear fell from his eyes, down his cheek. The nephew saw it and was shocked. He was so touched, he could not say a word. After that, even though he may have wanted to, the young man could not return to his old life.

STOP AND CONSIDER: What does it mean to truly accompany a person, with no judgment and no blame? Whom do you truly accompany? Can you accompany yourself?

To experience love and connection, to become free of fear, you must be willing to accept yourself and others just as you are; just as they are. You must be willing to let go of demands that others be a certain way, rejecting them if they are not. The Zen master could do that, and in accepting and living each moment fully, a spontaneously loving response occurred that allowed his nephew to grow naturally.

The natural is right,
The easy is right,
To be yourself is right.
To be yourself is all that you
Can really be,
Anything else is to go astray.

—*Bhagwan Shree Rajneesh*

The Road Home: Discovering Your Authentic Self

What else is needed to live from your authentic self, to be able to dip into your innate storehouse of courage and strength? A wonderful teaching from the Lankavatara Sutra (Buddhist teaching) helps answer this:

DON'T LOOK FOR WHAT IS REAL. JUST LET GO OF ALL THAT IS UNREAL, AND THAT WHICH IS REAL WILL COME TO YOU ALL BY ITSELF.

First you must become aware of the ways in which you cling to that which is not real—to toys and diversions. Often these provide a sense of self-worth. When you let go of that which is unreal, your authentic self will appear all by itself.

When we are little we play with toys. When we grow up we want the real thing.

—*Kosho Uchiyama Roshi, Zen master*

NOTICE how much time you spend each day escaping what would truly make you happy. Take note of how many times you offer a superficial, social response, not really looking, listening, speaking, or considering what is important to you. Do you see how this drains the meaning from your life, the joy out of your day?

WAKE UP. This is your life you are losing. You lose yourself daily in hundreds of tiny ways.

You make choices that harm you, decide to stay in deadening situations, and don't speak up about that which matters. You feel you have all the time in the world to wait for things to change. You don't. Fear tells you it is dangerous to be truthful. The real danger, however, is believing this fear and not discovering—or living—from your own truth.

The great American philosopher Ralph Waldo Emerson said: "When you have life in yourself, it is not by any known or appointed way; then you shall not discern the footsteps of any other. If we live truly, we shall see truly."

How many of us even know what it is that our heart treasures? How many have numbed ourselves so much that we've blocked it out? In order to truly be there for someone else, you must first learn how to be really there for yourself.

Restoring the Self

We are constantly invited to be who we are.

—Henry David Thoreau

There are many recovery groups these days: groups for alcohol issues, drug abuse, relationship abuse, sexual addiction, eating disorders, addictions of all kinds. How about recovery of the Self? Addictions and obsessions are fueled by hunger for the true Self and the emptiness of life without it. Once the Self is recovered, equilibrium is established, and everything else falls into place.

Becoming fearless requires that you recover your authentic self. The great advice of the Lankavatara Sutra suggests that you begin your journey to self-recovery by letting go of that which is false.

Of course, you can't do this until you've become aware of what is false in your life. For each of us it will be different. When one thing is let go of, then another will appear. You don't have to let go of everything at once. Just peel the onion little by little until you arrive at the core.

Mulla Nasrudin stood up in the marketplace and started to address the throng.

"Oh people! Do you want knowledge without difficulties, truth without falsehood, attainment without effort, progress without sacrifice?"

Very soon a large crowd gathered, everyone shouting: "Yes, yes!"

"Excellent!" said Nasrudin. "I only wanted to know. You may rely upon me to tell you all about it if I ever discover any such thing."

—*Indries Shah*

Who Are You? Who Are You Not?

In order to know who you are, you must also know who you are not, what is false and unworkable in your life, where you are living someone else's dream. You must know what feels disturbing, fundamentally out of sync with the person you are. It's important to acknowledge that which you *cannot* do, that which is *not* for you. So many of us spend years of our lives twisting ourselves out of shape to conform to other people's expectations of who we are or should become. Families and people who are "in love" are famous for projecting these images and demands upon one another. However, these expectations can be lethal. They cause pain, distortion, and lack of self-acceptance—the inability to know who we truly are.

TAKE A MOMENT to see what is natural, easy, and enjoyable for you; what actually brings enthusiasm about being alive.

Then take another moment to see what is not natural, easy, or enjoyable, what causes conflict, difficulty, confusion, and distress. What is it that pulls you down, hurts your feeling, upsets your digestion? Usually you do not give heed to this. Now is the time to turn it around. The first step is to take a good look. The next step is to say *No*.

You Can't Say Yes If You Can't Say No

This is a statement of truth and a great medicine that must be deeply absorbed. So much fear arises because you are unable to say no. I am not speaking of the impulsive, automatic no you offer out of resistance, anger, or stubbornness. I'm speaking of a different kind of no. It comes from understanding and accepting who you are and who you are *not*. It comes from knowing what is true for you and what is false. This no is a sign of respect for yourself, recognition that it is perfectly fine to be who you are; you do not have to disguise, distort, or reject your truth. You do not have to be all things to all people.

Many of us don't know what we should say no to. We feel guilty and ashamed of not "going along" with everything. We feel that if we don't meet everyone's needs, we've failed or there is something wrong with us. Some of us imagine that we should be able to belong everywhere, respond to every calling. But this scatters our forces and causes confusion. By living in this manner, we lose touch with our authentic Self and cannot develop the courage to be who we are.

If others reject you because you've said no, let them. (In chapter 5, you will learn how to reject rejection.) For now, realize that if you can't say no, you are rejecting your authentic self. Also, realize that if you can't say no, your yes is not a real one. It is an automatic, knee-jerk response. It arises out of obligation and the wish to be accepted. This is not a true yes, offered from the fullness of your being. If you can't offer a full, unconditional, unequivocal yes, then you are not living from your authentic Self. When you can say yes or no in an unconditional, wholehearted manner, fear has nowhere to stick.

Sometimes we receive the power to say Yes to life, then peace enters us and make us whole.

—*Ralph Waldo Emerson*

A great teacher, Soen Nakagawa Roshi, said that usually when we want to find beauty in a room, we bring in many fancy things—furniture, paintings, rugs, decorations. To find what we are looking for, however, it is better to take everything out of the room. When it is empty, its original beauty appears. When we take everything out of the room, we are saying no to whatever is in that the room that we don't want. We are emptying the room of all decoration to return to its original form.

TURNING POINT
You Are Granted Dominion in Your Own Life and World
Your life is a precious gift to you and to the world. No person, no thought, no emotion is granted dominion over you. You have ultimate power to choose the direction in which you want to go.

TWO

PRINCIPLE 2
Letting Go of Attachment and Grasping

Of all things, the most yielding can overcome the most strong.
—Tao Te Ching

We live with the incredible idea that everything will and should stay the same. We cling to this notion for dear life and are continually surprised when the things we love leave, wonderful relationships fade, our body changes, people behave in unexpected ways, and our fortunes fluctuate. When any of this happens, as it naturally must, we may even feel personally insulted or betrayed: "How can this be happening to me!" Others feel victimized by change, as if it's living proof that they are failures. They have "failed" to hold everything together, to keep things the same. They have "failed" to have their expectations realized—expectations that did not factor in the inevitable process of change.

A Taoist story tells of an old man who accidentally fell into the river rapids leading to a dangerous waterfall. Onlookers feared for his life. Miraculously, he came out alive and unharmed downstream, at the bottom of the falls. People asked him how he managed to survive.

He replied: "I accommodated myself to the water, not the water to me. Without thinking, I allowed myself to be shaped by it. Plunging into the swirl, I came out with the swirl. This is how I survived."

You Cannot Step into the Same River Twice

The Greek philosopher Heraclitus said, "You cannot step into the same river twice." The next moment you step into the river, not only is the river different, but you are different as well. Your body temperature has changed; your mood, the moment. Your cells are different, your thoughts, feelings, your understanding. You have been impacted by all that has happened to you. The river, too, has undergone changes: It has washed over rocks, swished the underbrush, tossed different fish inside it. Everything has altered the flowing stream. The river is different and so are you. How beautiful and thrilling.

However, many of us do not feel that change is beautiful and thrilling. We find it frightening, resist it, and do all we can to block it out. We set up dams to hold it back, using rigid beliefs and ideas to contain the flow.

But if not for the process of constant change, no growth would be possible. Your experience of yourself and others could not deepen. You would not be able to tell the difference between childish infatuation and real love. Without change, a child could not go from sitting to crawling, and then from crawling to walking. He would remain an infant forever. His life would not be fulfilled. Change is your friend. Change is a gift. It is crucial to learn to see it that way.

Fear, however, has a different plan. Fear says change is dangerous, and that security comes from holding on to what's familiar, to the past. The old ways are right, and new ways are wrong. You must hold on to what you learned in childhood, and what your family believed. Fear basically advises you not to grow up. Danish philosopher Søren Kierkegaard wisely said that most people never grow beyond fifteen years of age. They may grow chronologically, but not in other ways. They do not develop a sense of inquiry, inner independence, and openness to change. Instead they conform to old patterns and endlessly repeat the mistakes of the past.

The Repetition Compulsion

Sigmund Freud, the Austrian neurologist and founder of the psychoanalytic school of psychology, described a psychological phenomenon known as the repetition compulsion. This is the unconscious compulsion to repeat events or relationships that in the past were painful or traumatic, with which we have never really come to terms. When the repetition compulsion is operating, you automatically and unconsciously draw the same situation to yourself or relive the same relationship over and over again. Deep inside, you want it to turn out differently "this time." Usually, it doesn't. The situation can't turn out differently, however, because you aren't different; you are simply repeating the same old responses. Until you change, the rigidity of old patterns, beliefs, and expectations holds sway. When we are caught in the grip of the repetition compulsion, most of us become more and more distressed each time a situation or relationship is repeated and nothing different happens. Indries Shah presents many Sufi teachings in simple stories everyone can understand:

A man was sitting in front of a bowl of very sour pickles, eating one after another, and each time he bit into one, it was so sour it caused him to cry. He made a terrible face. His friend came by and saw him doing this.

"Why do you keep eating one sour pickle after another?" the friend asked.

"Because I'm waiting for a sweet one," the man said.

Like all of us, this man was doing the very same thing, over and over, hoping against hope that what was bitter and hard to take would suddenly become sweet. He kept experiencing bitterness rather than trying something else—finding a different kind of food. This man was caught in the repetition compulsion. He had become rigid, a prisoner of fear.

When fear dominates your life, it does not permit you to explore new possibilities. You live on automatic, never daring to walk away from your bowl of sour pickles or even consider that something sweet, delicious, and nourishing could be waiting a few steps away. Fear loves the repetition compulsion. It warns us to live only within our particular social, ethnic, or religious groups; to be wary of others. People who are different are considered dangerous. We must regard them with suspicion and keep them at arm's length.

A wonderful new family, with a different color skin, moves into an upscale neighborhood, excited to meet their new neighbors. A wave of alarm spreads over the neighborhood, however, and doors shut promptly. The people inside vigilantly guard themselves, their families, and their beliefs, never getting to know the newcomers and the gifts they've brought with them. Nor are the locals conscious of how much pain they cause the family.

When we cause pain, however, knowingly or unknowingly, we give fear a chance to grow. From deep within, we expect retaliation, or we find some ways to punish ourselves.

It's absolutely crucial to keep looking at the insidious ways fear distorts what could be a hopeful, joyous, thoroughly satisfying life into one of shut-up-ness and dread. As soon as you let a little light in, it is easy to notice that there are many cracks in fear's facade. There are many hidden doors, windows, and openings in what looks at first like a stone prison.

Change Is Not Loss

Dwelling as change itself brings peace.

—Buddhist teaching

Most of us resist change because it feels like loss. But change is not loss, it is simply change; it is inevitable, healthy, and necessary. Rather than seeing change as bringing new life and growth, it's easy to see it as a villain, taking something you've loved away. But if something truly belongs to you, nothing can take it away. If something does not belong to you, no matter how hard you cling to it, it still must go where it belongs.

LOOK AND SEE: What is it that you are holding on to right now? What do you refuse to let go of? You might not have even realized how hard you've been grasping it.

In the East, the concept of karma suggests that everyone comes into your life for a purpose, due to karma you have created, both in this life and previous ones. Karma is based on cause and effect. Your thoughts, deeds, and actions set up various causes, and sooner or later, when circumstances are ripe, the fruits of these causes appear in your life. They can come in almost any form—a new relationship, a job, illness, travel, what have you. The experience comes to help you grow, learn, and balance out previous karma you've set in motion. You are being given an opportunity to find a new, constructive way of responding to the old experience. Sometimes what comes is painful, but it is here so you can grow. Even if you receive a positive experience—for example, a loving relationship—it can stay for only a designated amount of time. Holding on, attaching, grasping, is entirely futile and counterproductive.

All composite things must, one day, decompose.

—*Diamond Sutra*

Life has its own intrinsic laws of coming and going, meeting and parting. Once you have met and shared another person's life, you become a part of each other, always connected; there is nothing you can lose. By letting go, throughout all your experiences, you can enjoy what comes more fully, learn lessons more quickly, and not create more negative karma to be balanced out in the future.

Two Zen monks were in the forest when they saw a beautiful woman in distress. She was lost and needed help finding her way home. They took her along with them and soon came to a deep stream. One of the monks picked her up and carried her across. After they crossed the stream, he put her down and guided her to the right road.

The two monks continued walking. Finally, after about an hour, one monk said to the one who had lifted the woman, "You know, we are not allowed to touch a woman. Yet you picked that woman up and carried her in your arms."

"Yes, I did," said the other monk. "But I have put her down, and you are still carrying her with you now."

When you put down whatever you have been carrying, you can walk along freely without guilt and obstructions. Physically, it may be easy to put a woman down, but more difficult to drop the thoughts and fantasies you carry about her. Yet the more we put down of our inner baggage, the lighter and freer our trip through life will be.

When They Come We Welcome, When They Go We Do Not Pursue

When you take your hands off life and allow it to run its natural course, not only do you receive many wonderful surprises, but a great deal of energy and peace of mind are restored.

WELCOME WHATEVER COMES into your world today, even if you didn't plan for it or it seems unwanted; welcome it if it is there. Don't fight it off. Instead, thank it for being present. As you do so, you will become available to experience whatever happens in a truly different way.

WHEN SOMETHING LEAVES, don't hold on. Let it go, thank it for the time you spent together, and give it space to go, without guilt, sorrow, or dread. This is giving a very great gift.

When it's time for something to go, it has to go. Honor that. You cannot change the natural cycles and rhythm of life. By realizing that what comes to you is temporary, that life is nothing but a flow, a great deal of fear and pain are averted.

Become Complete

Take your full time to drink your cup of tea.

—*Lojong teachings, Tibetan Buddhism*

It's difficult to let someone you love go when you do not feel complete, when you feel you've left something unsaid or undone. Perhaps you had dreams about the relationship that were never fulfilled. Or maybe you were not really present in the relationship, didn't experience it 100 percent, or didn't give it everything you could have given it—or receive everything in return. This is especially painful when it comes time to die. Some say it is not dying that is so hard, but the pain of a life that has not been lived.

When you have lived your life fully, tasted each experience, you feel full and complete. You will have drunk your cup of tea to the very last drop. Then, when it is time for you to go, you will not grieve for what was left undone. And you will be ready for what the next moment brings.

Feeding the Hungry Ghost

Some people are unable to feel full and complete. They crave so much that no matter what they have, they cannot be satisfied. This is called being a hungry ghost, being run by the affliction of greed. When a hungry ghost is invited to a banquet, he samples everything, eats it up, but cannot taste, savor, or digest the delicious meal in front of him. No matter what he eats, he is left hungrier than before.

Similarly, when a hungry ghost is invited to the banquet of life, he cannot taste or digest his experiences. A hungry ghost can be hungry for food, love, money, sex, recognition, anything. Whatever he receives, he wants more. The hungry ghost does not realize that it is greed that causes the pain. And the more he grasps, the more he crushes whatever he has in the palm of his hand. As you learn to let go, rather than feed your cravings, the hunger and fear will start to subside.

The Disease of the Mind

> To separate what we like
> From what we dislike
> Is the disease of the mind.
>
> —*Zen Master Sosan*

As you feed your cravings, you become controlled by the desire to search for and cling to whatever feels good and reject whatever feels threatening. When you find what you like, you become attached; when you find what you dislike, you use all your power to push it away. Thus, you spend your precious life energy discarding half your experience and grasping at and clinging to the rest. Living in this way, you become completely dependent on external conditions for your sense of well-being. A sunny day will make you happy, but as soon as thunderstorms arrive, your happiness is gone. Like a leaf blowing in the wind, you can't relax, and you're always on guard about what's coming next. Because people and conditions constantly change, you have no idea what you can really hold on to or where to find true security.

> A student went to his meditation teacher and said, "My meditation is horrible, I feel so distracted, my legs ache, and I am constantly falling asleep."
> "It will pass," the teacher said matter-of-factly.
> A week later, the student came back to his teacher. "My meditation is wonderful! I feel so aware, so peaceful, so alive!"
> "It will pass," the teacher said matter-of-factly, again.
>
> —*Zen teaching*

You may think something painful is bad for you, and something that feels good is positive. But this is not so. You may be rejecting something that could be meaningful, because it makes you uneasy initially. You may be staying attached to something that is harmful, simply because it is familiar. It's impossible to realize what is truly beneficial when you live in this way.

NOTICE: What is it you chase after and hold on to for dear life? What is it you routinely avoid, reject, or hide from? Can you see what a toll this takes on you? Does this way of being bring comfort, safety, or happiness? Be honest with yourself. That's all that's needed now, honesty.

When you begin to let go, to open your hands, mind, heart, you reverse this age-old pattern. You begin to see that what you like or dislike is not a measure of anything. You cannot base your life on it. Often you dislike something because you know nothing about it, and you recoil from something that may be entirely good. Beyond that, your likes and dislikes are constantly changing. One day, something that you adored may cause you to recoil.

As you undertake the process of dissolving fear, do not separate what you like from what you dislike; don't chase after one thing and reject another. Instead, slowly open your mind and hands to everything.

When Dogen, a great Zen master, was young, he went to China to study Zen. Dogen spent many years there, and then undertook a dangerous journey back to Japan. When he reached his homeland, many people had heard about him and came to see him. When they asked him what he had learned during all those years in the monastery, he said, "I came back with nothing but empty hands."

Empty hands are precious. When your hands are empty, not grasping, they become supple and available. They can feel, they can touch, reach out to others, give and accept gifts in return. Dogen's open hands were available to all of life. He was not holding on to what he liked and pushing the rest away. He was willing to accept and be with it all.

EMPTY YOUR HANDS. What are you holding on to tightly? Can you open your hands for a moment and let it go? Can you stop grasping that which you desire and pushing away what may not feel good? See yourself opening your hands and allowing something to go. See yourself opening a fist you may have clenched to fight or reject part of life. Stop fighting and allow it to be.

Instead of Rejecting Life, Reject Fear

Deep within ourselves, we do not allow life to be what it is. We judge, condemn, and refuse life in many subtle ways. Fear enjoys harming life. Do not go along with its destructive wishes. There is never, ever anything good that comes out of creating harm. Extricate yourself from this activity. Claim a different desire. When you feel the desire to harm or reject, realize this desire does not belong to you. It belongs to fear. You do not have to go along with fear's madness.

Turn to fear and say No. Instead of rejecting life, reject fear.

The process of learning to say no is one of the most powerful medicines you have against fear. There are many ways you can use this medicine. For now, say no to grasping and unhealthy attachment. Practice opening your hands, your mind, your heart. As you do so, you are restoring yourself to flexibility, spontaneity, and real security. Say no to rigidity. Once you open your hands and let go, you will be amazed to see all the wonderful new people, experiences, and inner freedom that come into your life.

There is a wonderful Zen story about a great teacher who was wholly able to let go. When something came he welcomed it; when it left he did not pursue it:

> There was a great teacher who lived in a small village, where he was highly revered. He spent time alone meditating. The villagers thought he was a great, holy person and brought him food and other offerings. Everyone spoke of him highly. He lived safely and simply.
>
> Then suddenly one day a young woman from the village found herself pregnant, and the father of the child said he was going to leave. He wasn't ready to be a father or to care for her. With no one to turn to, and filled with despair, the young woman told the villagers that the great teacher was the father of the baby. When the teacher heard about this, all he said was, "Is that so?"
>
> The villagers were horrified. Their feelings about the teacher changed entirely. Their faces grew dark when his name was mentioned. They spoke ill of him, and no longer visited or brought him food. When the teacher heard about how he was being slandered, all he said was, "Is that so?"
>
> After the baby was born, the young woman brought the child to the teacher and said, "Here, take your baby."
>
> "Is that so?" the teacher replied, and with loving, outstretched arms, he reached for the child and took it.
>
> The teacher cared for the child with great devotion for several

years. Then suddenly one day the real father returned to the village. He had great remorse for having left and wanted to be reunited with and care for the young woman and child. Thrilled, the young woman told the entire village the truth about what had happened. Then she and the young man went to the teacher to claim their child.

"Is that so?" the teacher said, and lovingly returned the child to his parents.

Now the entire village had nothing but praise for the teacher. When they spoke of him, their faces shone. They returned to his cottage, bringing gifts and food.

"Is that so?" the teacher said and accepted the gifts lovingly.

This great teacher was not at all affected by passing conditions, of praise or blame, receiving or losing. He was fearless, completely able to accept whatever came to him, and also willing to let go when the time came.

"Is that so?" is a practice. It is a way of responding to events that seem good and those that seem bad, those that bring pleasure and those that bring pain. Rather than jump on the roller coaster of life, take the ride, enjoy the thrills, and then crash when the ride is over, the teacher remained fully centered within his own being and did not allow passing conditions to hold sway over him. He knew that all is transient, that good turns to bad, bad turns to good, pleasure to pain, pain to pleasure. By remaining centered, by simply watching all of life with interest, by accepting and caring for whatever came, he was free from fear about what happened. He was also free of longing for praise and fearing blame. With no grasping or attachment, he was completely secure, able to love fully, to care for whatever came to him, and to part with it when it had to go.

Pinpointing Fear

If you look more closely at the behavior of the great teacher, it is easy to see the causes of fear, and how to become free of them. In this case, if the great teacher had struggled to defend his reputation, if he'd harbored hate and resentment toward the villagers for what they once gave and then took away, his pain would have intensified. He refused hate, blame, and resentment, however, all of which are fuels for fear.

If the great teacher had refused to accept the child who was given, or had turned the young woman away, not only would his thoughts have returned to both of them, but he would have caused greater consternation in the village, his life surrounded by uproar. By accepting all that came to him, he lived in harmony, thus undoing the rise of fear in others and himself.

When the time came to let go, if the great teacher had clung to the child and refused to return it, if he hadn't known how to give back the gifts given to him, once again pain and fear would reign. By knowing that nothing belonged to him, that all came for a while and had to go, he dismantled the grip of fear of loss and thus remained in deep balance.

The great teacher had learned how to live with open hands. He saw the profound transience of life. This fact did not make him sad; rather, it freed him to live in wonder and peace. Rather than being attached to a particular outcome, he let life happen as it would. He did not harbor any particular agenda for how life had to unfold. He did not hold on to a specific notion of his role in life, of the honors due him, of how important he was and what he deserved. Relinquishing attachment did not mean he was unable to love. In fact, only by letting go was he fully able to give himself. The great teacher had found a place of true security that could never be threatened.

Your Escape from Fear

Perhaps the great teacher seems superhuman. He is not. He is as human as all of us—he just understands the basic principles of peace of mind and lives in their light. You, too, can learn these principles and practice them daily. This entire book is an escape from fear. Each exercise, suggestion, and statement of truth brings more light into the darkness that fear creates. You just need to keep the light shining. You might shine it for a moment or two, see a way out, and then become afraid. That's natural. But keep the light shining. Bring more and more light in.

When fear comes, stop, look at it, breathe it in, and then breathe it out. Find one of the exercises that resonates with you, and do it on the spot. The means of escape, the cracks in the wall, will become larger and larger; the attacks of fear weaker and fewer. The lies that fear tells will fade away.

Alex started his escape from fear and his life began to open up. People were more available to him, he began having insights about which actions to take, and on many days he actually felt good. Then he suddenly froze up. He said it was scary that this was so easy, and he wanted to hold on to the way things were for a little while longer. For a while he retreated into the pseudo-safety of escape. But he'd had a taste of something different. His escape didn't last as long. Deep down he knew there was a way out.

Why is it frightening to escape from fear? Because if you let it go, you may wonder what will keep you safe and secure. You believe that the more frightened you are, the more alert you will be to danger. The more you keep everything the same, the more stable your life will be.

The opposite is true. Fear freezes you up, and as you grow stiffer you become more dead than alive. A corpse is stiff and unyielding. A live person is flexible and spontaneous, flows with changing conditions, and is able to give and take freely . . . to open his hands and let go.

WHAT ARE YOU HOLDING ON TO and grasping, as if for dear life? For now, just notice. Notice the ways in which you refuse to allow change. What is this doing to those you love? What is it doing to you? Just keep noticing.

By refusing to let go, you are fighting against the force of change. Of course, this force has to win. No one can stop the tide from coming in and flowing out. No one can keep the sun from rising in the morning and setting at night. Who would waste their precious life energy this way? And yet we struggle with the tide of events, people, beliefs, thoughts, and desires that come to us, and that naturally will go. We rail against ourselves, against others and God. We vow never to love again or care about anything. This is certainly a form of insanity, fueled by fear.

Fear loves insanity. It teaches insanity, is insane itself. It confuses the mind in thousands of ways. However, each time you see that which is insane, as insane, your sanity is restored. It is reckless to live in an insane manner and foolish to refuse to face the reality you live in. It is also understandable that you do so. T. S. Eliot has described this condition beautifully: "Human beings cannot bear very much reality."

Why is that? Because fear has invaded all of our being. We cannot even bear to taste the reality that would take us out of prison and cause our fear to melt away.

There is an old Chinese tale about a woman whose only son died. In her grief, she went to the holy man and said, "What prayers or incantations do you know that may bring my child back to life?"

He simply said, "Bring me a mustard seed from a home that has never known sorrow. We will use it to drive the sorrow out of your life." The woman went off at once in search of that magical mustard seed.

She first came to a splendid mansion, knocked at the door, and said, "I am looking for a home that has never known sorrow. Is this such a home?"

They said, "You've certainly come to the wrong place." Then they began to describe all the tragic events that had recently befallen them.

The woman said to herself, *Who is better able to help these poor unfortunate people than I, who have had such misfortune of my own?* She stayed to comfort them, and then went on in search of a home that had never known sorrow. But wherever she turned, in hovels and beautiful places, she found one tale after another of sadness and misfortune. She became so involved in ministering to other people's grief that ultimately she forgot about her quest for the magical mustard seed, never realizing that caring for others had driven the sorrow out of her life.

Reality Is Entirely Good

Despite the false rumors that fear whispers, reality is entirely good. This may seem like a shocking statement. You have been taught to see reality as dangerous and fear as good. Turn this madness on its ear. How could you survive, grow, thrive, love, laugh, worship, if the fundamental reality you were born from were not entirely good? How could you be able to see great beauty, eat a meal when hungry, or hold the hand of a friend? Who is it that has turned this banquet into a meager meal? Who is it that looks at life with a malevolent eye?

FIND WAYS in which life is good; ways it has given to you, supported you, nourished you. Have you offered thanks? Have you given to, supported, and nourished life? Have you accepted the great gifts offered, or have you said No to them?

The Rejection-of-Life Compulsion

Along with the repetition compulsion, there is what I call the rejection-of-life compulsion. You reject life in many ways and then feel as though life is rejecting you. One of the main fuels for the rejection-of-life compulsion is the refusal to face reality. How happy you will be when you turn this around.

Many of us refuse to taste reality because we fear that we'll taste something wonderful and then it will be gone. But although one taste may be over, there's another one right there, waiting. And each taste is delicious, as long as you do not always compare it with the taste before, or the one yet to come. Transience is not something to fear, but rather to be wholly entered into and enjoyed.

We are here for a short time and then we depart. This can be the cause of fear or the impetus for living a clear and beautiful life. This realization can make each day more precious and can place what is truly important in clear perspective. Facing and accepting transience, you relish each encounter. Above all, this acceptance can strengthen your resolve not to allow the precious time you have to be co-opted by fear.

Transience cannot be guarded against. It is a basic truth of life. When it is seen and adopted fully, everything starts to change. We hide from the fear of transience by holding on, unwilling to let go. We hide by making everything seem solid and important, as if our very life depended on it. We act as if our life depended upon relationships, money, status, and accomplishments. It does not. Our life depends on something else. When you discover what your life truly depends upon, then you become completely free of fear.

This Transient World

Thus shall ye think of this fleeting world,
A star at dawn, a bubble in a stream;
A flash of lightning in a summer cloud
A flickering lamp, a phantom, and a dream.

—*Diamond Sutra*

Change and loss are your teachers. When you experience difficult losses, take it as an opportunity to deepen your willingness to become truly available to those in your life. Take it as a time to express the love you've been holding inside. In the interview that follows with Sue Matthews, the brave and beautiful mother of Taylor Matthews, we see these principles manifested in so many ways.

In 2003, when my beautiful, spirited daughter Taylor was 11 years old, I took her for a routine physical examination, and we discovered, to our shock, a large tumor between her ribs. Soon after, we learned that the cancer had metastasized. It was all over. Taylor was given three months to live.

Our whole world turned upside down. Our home became her bedside at the hospital, where I lived, breathed, and slept constantly. We were going to try everything. Surrounded by prayers and love, Taylor began to undergo surgeries, chemotherapy, radiation, the works.

I had no idea how I could go on or face this terrible ordeal, but Taylor taught me. Her spirit was indomitable. No matter what she went through, I never heard her complain. She took whatever came and had no intention of letting the cancer get her down or stopping her from living life to the last drop. When I became sad, she'd focus on something fun or exciting and put my attention on that. Taylor loved life and intended to live it completely, no matter how much time she did or didn't have. Over and over she reminded me, "Mom, this is a life worth living."

We all became part of a new family—the children and parents on the cancer floor. Taylor loved her constant friends and companions, would prowl around the halls, pulling her IVs with her, looking for someone to play with and cheer up. She hated it when kids just lay in bed sad, staring at TV. She'd race up and down the halls in her wheelchair, getting games going. There was so much to do, so much fun to have.

At her young age, she became too familiar with loss. She saw many of the little friends she grew to love die. As this happened, Taylor became more and more determined to find some way to help. Before long she began to design bracelets and bands, called tay-bandz, to sell and donate the money for pediatric cancer research. Next step was to start a foundation. Taylor arranged for fashion shows, walks, events, and all kinds of activities to raise the money. Over the next five years, the foundation raised just about a million dollars for cancer research on kids. All she talked about was helping everyone else.

Taylor refused to see herself as a sick person. Even while she was undergoing treatment and throwing up, she wouldn't let that stop her from doing things that meant a lot. And she wouldn't let her cancer stop her from being the mischievous little girl she was. One time, after massive lung surgery, she was told she had to walk the floor twice in one day. Taylor walked the floor once. The night nurses then came in, checking up. When they heard she'd only walked the floor once, they insisted that she get up and do it again.

"Who wants to walk a hospital floor again?" she said to her dad, who was sitting there. "I'm walking right out of the hospital." She got up out of bed and walked straight to the elevator instead. Then she and her father got on the elevator and walked out onto 62nd Street and York Avenue and headed straight down to Ben & Jerry's and had some ice cream instead.

Another time, fourteen days after spine fusion surgery, Taylor announced, "I'm going on vacation with my sister waterskiing!"

"Waterskiing?" I said, "Fourteen days after surgery? How's that possible? You just had a spine fusion. It can't be done."

"Why not?" Taylor said. In her world everything was possible.

I didn't want to be the one to stop her. "Ask the doctor," I said, thinking that he would tell her how crazy the idea was.

We called her surgeon and to my amazement he said, "Taylor, if you feel you can do it, go right ahead."

She went, water-skied, and had a wonderful time.

Taylor would not allow the illness to become center stage in her life. It was just a fact of life, an annoyance, something you dealt with while you were doing other exciting things. Despite chemotherapy, radiation, and all the aftereffects, she didn't let a moment slip by where she could help someone, work on her foundation, or just plain enjoy herself.

Despite her grim diagnosis, she beat the odds. When she was twelve and a half until fourteen and a half, Taylor's cancer went into remission. She lived for five years, until she was sixteen years old, not three months as originally predicted.

During those precious five years, Taylor did not miss out on a drop. When she was out of the hospital, she went to school, spent time with good friends, had a wonderful boyfriend, Jason, whom she adored and who adored her as well. She drove a convertible, took her SATs, and two weeks before she died took off her oxygen as she went for her college tour and interview at Brown. After the interview, gasping for air, she grabbed it and put it on, triumphant that she had been able to go. Taylor had no idea the end was near. She fully expected to attend college. She always focused upon what lay ahead.

She only talked with us about dying one time. It was very early on. As she and her dad were eating pizza, she asked, "Dad, am I going to die?"

"Everybody dies, Taylor," her dad said. "That's the way it is."

—*From an unpublished interview conducted by the author with Sue Matthews*

And it's true that everyone dies, but does everyone live? Really live as Taylor did?

TURNING POINT

You Can't Step into the Same River Twice

Recognize the fleeting nature of life. Make peace with it. Spend time watching changes that take place naturally, and embrace the beauty within these changes. See how each change brings something new in its wake.

Make a practice of enjoying change, welcoming it into your life. If you notice catastrophic expectations cropping up, say no to them. Focus on whatever life is giving. Realize that these expectations are just fear rising, trying to keep itself alive.

THREE

PRINCIPLE 3

Recognizing the Voices Within

Where is the road to Hanshan?
There is no road to Hanshan.
—Zen saying

WHEN UNEXPECTED EVENTS COME INTO YOUR LIFE, it's easy to lose your bearings. Unprepared for sudden change and gripped by fear, the world no longer seems safe or secure. You wonder when the next shoe is going to fall . . . and whom you can really trust. You may feel you can't depend on others—or on yourself, for that matter. When your certainty is shaken, it can be difficult to determine what is real and what is not. At this juncture, it's easy to retreat into fantasies. The truth is that although these fantasies seem to bring comfort, they disconnect you from what is actually happening, from workable solutions and true peace of mind.

Mirages and Dreams

The world of fantasies is a world all of us live in, automatically and unknowingly. As soon as something happens that is difficult to cope with—a desire obstructed, a relationship threatened—we retreat into fantasies in order to regain equilibrium and get power over our world.

These fantasies have many functions. On the surface, they seem to comfort, soothe hurt feelings, calm temporarily, and make you feel that all is well. Some fantasies create an explanation for what might have happened. Others provide wished-for outcomes, as though the situation is being handled and you are victorious. Usually, in your fantasies, you are vindicated, a winner. You find the love you've been looking for, reclaim your pride, do away with enemies.

In other fantasies, you may see yourself as a hapless victim. These fantasies reinforce negative beliefs, distorting the reality of who you are and what has really gone on.

This Sufi story shows the harmful power of living in fantasies and false expectations:

A woman named Truhana, not being very rich, had to go yearly to the market to sell honey. As she walked on, carrying the jar of honey on her head, she calculated how much money she would get for it. *First,* she thought, *I will sell it and buy eggs. Then I'll put the eggs under my fat brown hens and in time there will be plenty of little chicks. Soon these chicks will become chickens and from the sale of these, lambs can be bought.*

Then Truhana started to imagine how she could become richer than her neighbors and how she could marry off her sons and daughters to mates who were wealthy as well.

Trudging along in the hot sun, she could see her fine sons and daughters-in-laws and how people would say it was remarkable how rich she had become, she who was once so poverty-stricken.

Under the influence of these pleasurable thoughts, she began to laugh heartily and preen herself, when suddenly striking the jar with her hand it fell from her head and smashed on the ground. The honey became a sticky mess on the ground.

Seeing this, Truhana suddenly became as depressed as she had been excited, seeing that her dreams were now lost and realizing that they were only illusion.

Dwelling in fantasies is dangerous. Although they may seem to be a comfort initially, they are based on fear. Because they draw you away from reality, keeping your energies tied up in wishful thinking, the basic situation that has caused your upset is never faced. In fact, because it is not being attended to, the situation often intensifies, festers, and grows.

THINK OF a situation you do not feel you can handle. What kind of dreams, fantasies, and mirages do you substitute instead? What are these fantasies really doing for you? Does anything in your life change or improve because of them? Are you even aware of when you are lost in a dream?

Is your favorite fantasy one of pleasure, or does it make you fearful? By getting in touch with what your habitual fantasies are, you can learn more about what haven't faced in your life, what it is you fear. When you discover the underlying problem, then face and handle it constructively, your fantasies will subside.

A Fantasy Is a Fantasy

Fantasies can feel like reality because of their intensity, and when you replay them over and over again they begin to feel like old friends. When fantasies become this familiar, you can become oblivious to the many warnings, signs, and messages that life is sending you about the truth of the situation you happen to be in. Then, when things escalate, when the harsh truth appears and you're suddenly fired, or your relationship abruptly ends, the shock can be enormous. You had no idea this was coming because you simply weren't available to really hear or see what was going on in your own life.

> Lou was crazy about Mara and heard her say that she loved him as well. He was on cloud nine, telling his friends that an engagement was just around the corner. Lou did not actually hear what Mara was truly saying or the tone of voice she spoke in. In actuality, Mara said to him sadly that she could love him one day if she ever felt that he would learn how to listen to her and understand what she was feeling. The gist of her communication was that she thought the day would never come, and she felt sad about it.

When a relationship ends suddenly, so many people say to the partner, "I told you how I felt over and over and you never heard me. You blocked me out."

Becoming Deaf and Blind

By drawing your attention away from the actual situation, fantasies make you deaf and blind. No matter what is in front of your eyes, you cannot see it. You see only your fantasy about it. No matter what is being said, you don't really hear. You may hear only a portion of what is being communicated and may distort the rest. Your fantasies filter in information you want to hear and filter out whatever doesn't fit in with your desires.

A huge part of becoming fearless is developing the ability to recognize what reality brings you and not get lost in a mirage. When you are able to actually register what's happening, you will simultaneously find real ways of responding to what's being asked of you.

Indries Shah's story about the Sufi sage Nasrudin shows how reality easily gets confused:

> Nasrudin went to see a rich man.
> "Give me some money," he said.
> "Why?" asked the rich man.
> "I want to buy—an elephant."
> "If you have no money, you can't afford to keep an elephant," said the rich man.
> "I came here," said Nasrudin, "to get money, not advice."

Every day reality brings opportunities, guidance, and unexpected gifts. Are you available to receive them, or are you lost in a fantasy about what should happen, how the world should treat you?

MAKE A LIST of the underlying situations that need to be handled in your life. Just by becoming aware of them and writing them down, the fear about them will subside. When you keep needs repressed and disguised, fear does not go away—instead it grows stronger.

Obsessive-Compulsive Behavior

When fantasies take over, obsessive thinking is not far behind. Obsessive, repetitive thinking is designed to tie you in a knot. When you're caught in the grip of obsessive thinking—in an attempt to come to terms with the blows you've been dealt or to ensure that all will go as you wish in the future—your mind replays the same events over and over again, never finding a solution.

Obsessive thinking develops naturally into obsessive-compulsive behavior. Rather than face the reality of how out of control you feel, you now substitute repetitive behaviors and rituals to produce a feeling of stability and safety. The price you pay for this is enormous: Repetitive behaviors not only limit your life, they take enormous time and energy to keep going. They take your freedom away, and the sense of safety they produce is fragile. As soon as a ritual is not performed, or a certain behavior not engaged in, guilt or fear arises once again.

Lisa could not forgive either herself or her father for the terrible abuse she had suffered at his hands. She had no idea, either, how to cleanse herself or feel worthwhile again. At first, she began washing her hands after every meal, feeling it wiped the shame away. Soon, it wasn't enough to wash after every meal; she began washing between meals as well. That felt even better, but when she forgot to do it, anxiety arose. Before long, she also had to wash whenever she was out in public. The compulsion was taking control of her life, and she felt terrified when she forgot. Lisa couldn't understand why the more she washed, the more she needed to.

Obsessive-compulsive rituals soothe anxiety temporarily. But unless the source of the anxiety is faced and released, it remains, lurking beneath the surface. Lisa's compulsion was a defense against feelings she had related to the abuse. She had no idea how to free herself from these feelings and was symbolically washing away the pain she felt. In the long run, however, as obsessive behavior and rituals take over, they restrict and impair our lives and fuel addictions of all kinds. Ultimately, they cause more anxiety and loss of control.

To a degree, all of us seek to control fear through fantasies, routines, rituals, and automatic patterns that we can't seem to let go of. The more we indulge them, however, the more frightening reality can seem, and the less able we are to take effective action. But remember: You are stronger than all of your compulsive behaviors. You can stop, you can decide, you can choose to take different action. Here is a wonderful exercise to help undo obsessions and compulsions of all kinds.

Just Do It

You can't cross a sea by merely staring into the water.

—*Rabindranath Tagore*

Just do it. Take action. Get up, get out, engage with life, and *do something. Take one step and then the next, no matter how you feel.* Fear will fight you on this. It will tell you to wait, think it over, hide, get ready, prepare, postpone—make sure all conditions are perfectly set. Of course, conditions are never all perfectly set. That day will never come. Fear tells you you're not ready, be careful, you'll fall down, make a fool of yourself.

SAY TO THE FEAR: "What's wrong with falling down, being wrong, making a fool of myself? Nothing. It's not nearly as dangerous as living immobilized." Who is ever really ready for anything? If you wait until you're ready, you stay locked in fantasy and nothing happens.

BY TAKING ACTION YOU BECOME READY.

FIND ONE ACTION you hesitate to take, and just do it now. Stop everything else, stop thinking, just get up and do it now. Once you are in action, the next steps come more easily, and you can then clearly see what is needed next.

By taking action in the present moment, you learn, grow, and discover your own enormous power. You discover the consequence of your choices and can make new, wiser choices. What difference does it make if you succeed or fail? By living in total fear of failure, you live in the grip of fear.

Here's a wonderful story for anyone who compulsively wonders when and what to do, and with whom.

One day an emperor decided that if he knew the answer to three questions, he would always know what to do, no matter what, and wouldn't have to wonder over and over. So he made an announcement throughout the kingdom that if anyone could answer his three questions, he would give them a big reward.

The questions were:

When is the best time to do things?

Who are the most important people?

What is the most important thing?

The emperor received many answers but was unsatisfied. Finally, he traveled to a mountain to visit a wise hermit who lived at the top. When he arrived, he asked his three questions. The hermit, who was digging in his garden, listened carefully and then returned to digging without saying a word. As the hermit continued digging, the emperor noticed how tired the old man seemed.

"Here," he said, "give me the spade. I'll dig and you can rest a bit."

So the hermit rested while the emperor dug.

After digging for several hours, the emperor was very tired. He said, "If you can't answer my questions, just tell me, and I'll leave."

"Do you hear someone running?" asked the hermit suddenly, pointing to the edge of the woods. And, sure enough, a man came tumbling out of the woods clutching his stomach. He collapsed as the hermit and emperor reached him. Then they saw that he had a deep cut. The emperor cleaned the wound, using his own shirt to bind it. The man awoke and asked for water. The emperor hurried to a nearby stream and brought him some. The man drank gratefully, then slept.

The hermit and emperor carried the man into the hut and lay him on the hermit's bed. By then the emperor, too, was exhausted and fell asleep.

The next morning, when the emperor awoke, the wounded man was staring down at him. "Forgive me," the man whispered.

"Forgive you?" said the emperor, sitting up, wide awake. "What have you done that needs my forgiveness?"

"You do not know me, Your Majesty, but I have thought of you as my sworn enemy. During the war, you killed my brother and took away my lands. So I swore vengeance and vowed to kill you. And yesterday, I was lying in ambush waiting for you, but for some reason you didn't return. So I left my hiding place to find you. Instead, your attendants found me and, recognizing me, attacked, giving me a painful wound.

"I fled, but if you hadn't helped me when you did, I would have died. You saved my life. I am ashamed and very grateful. Please forgive me."

The emperor was astonished. "I am sorry for the pain I caused you," he said. "Let us be friends from this time on."

After the man left, the emperor turned to the hermit. "I must leave now," he said, "and find the answers to my three questions."

The hermit laughed and said, "Your questions are already answered. If you had not helped me dig my garden yesterday, delaying your return, you would have been attacked on your way home. Therefore, the most important time for you was the time you were digging in my garden. The most important person was myself, the person you were with, and the most important pursuit was simply to help me.

"Later, when the wounded man came, the most important time was the time you spent tending to his wound, for otherwise he would have died and you would have lost forever the opportunity for forgiveness and friendship. At that moment, he was the most important person, and the most important pursuit was tending his wound.

"The present moment is the only moment," said the hermit. "The most important person is always the person you are with. And the most important pursuit is making the person standing at your side happy. What could be simpler or more important?"

The emperor bowed in gratitude to the old teacher and left in peace.

—*From* One Hand Clapping: Zen Stories for All Ages,
as retold by Rafe Martin and Manuela Soares

Mistakes Are Your Friend

It's easy to understand why it's so difficult to act when you're so fearful of making mistakes. However, there's nothing wrong with making mistakes. After all, mistakes are your friend. You can't get up if you don't fall down. No child would ever walk if she feared falling down. It is natural to fall and get up again. It is natural to take action, learn from what happens, strengthen your muscles, and move forward. You can't move forward if you fear failure or making mistakes. In fact, it's good to make a so-called mistake. It means you've taken a risk. You've stood up to fear and became stronger than it. A great teacher, Dogen, said,

"LIFE IS ONE CONTINUOUS MISTAKE."

Anything that makes you stronger than fear, anytime you stand up to the bully, take a risk, look fear in the eye, and take action, you have won. It doesn't matter how things turn out. You have lessened fear's hold on you and reclaimed your original freedom.

If you fall down a hundred times, that means you have won a hundred times. You have faced fear one hundred times, gotten up, and tried again. You have strengthened yourself in the process and weakened fear. You have reclaimed the truth of who you are and emerged completely more powerful than fear.

TAKE A LOOK at the times you made a mistake, fell down. Describe what happened. What did you learn from it? What did you fail to learn? Write down what you thought should have happened.

It's easy to call something a mistake because the outcome is something you didn't expect, or because it caused you pain. But who's deciding it was a mistake? If the outcome had been different, would it have been okay?

You decide a mistake is a mistake. But it's just something that happened and turned out a certain way. Why even call it a mistake? Because you weren't able to control all aspects of life? Who can? Why should you?

It is fascinating to see how strong the fear of being wrong is, and how strong the longing to be perfect all the time. These feelings are embedded in fantasy and are the voice of fear. Turn a deaf ear to this foolish voice and enjoy being wrong whenever you are.

> "There are some things," said Nasrudin, "that you positively know inwardly must be untrue."
> "Can I have an example?" asked someone who was always looking for evidence.
> "Certainly. For instance, the other day when I was walking along, I heard a rumor that I was dead."
>
> —*Indries Shah*

What's Wrong with Being Wrong?

WHAT'S WRONG with being wrong? Write down all the times you were wrong. Who cared? What happened? Was it the end of the world? Did you learn something from being wrong?

List five ways you can be wrong now. Do one each day. See what happens? Is it so terrible? Do you want to live your life terrified of being wrong?

By being so afraid of being wrong and insisting on always being right, you drive yourself crazy. You drive others crazy as well; if you feel they're wrong, you dismiss or reject them. Or if you imagine that someone else is right and you're wrong, you feel inadequate. Living in this manner, you are firmly caught in a mirage.

Mirages aren't only in the desert—life is filled with them. When you drive in the desert and see a non-existent lake up ahead, it looks completely real. But it's just an illusion created by your thirst. Thinking it is real, however, you race ahead to drink from it. The more you race toward the mirage, the farther it recedes. Then it seems that the water is a few hundred feet up ahead. You race even farther in the hot desert, intensifying your thirst and becoming even more desperate for water. But this mirage—or any mirage, for that matter—will never quench your thirst. The fantasy of being a perfect person, who is always right and not permitted to be wrong, is simply a mirage. Searching for perfection will drive you crazy and never bring wisdom or fulfillment into your life.

Nothing will break this defeating pattern until you acknowledge that a mirage is a mirage. It doesn't exist; you've made it up. The same applies to your race toward perfection and fear of doing anything wrong. Life is one continuous course of action, reaction, and more action, where the most important thing is: Do what you can do, as fully as you can, with your whole heart. Be as available to reality as you can be—see, hear, and feel clearly—and then respond. When you take wholehearted action, your life changes, and step by step you come out of hiding and remember who you are. The consequences of your actions are not your business. Just take each step wholeheartedly and see what happens.

There was once a prince who took ill and decided he was a turkey. He stripped off his clothing and crouched naked under the royal table, refusing to eat anything but crumbs that had fallen to the floor. The king was greatly upset. Many doctors were called to the palace to examine the prince, but none could offer a cure.

One day a wise man came to the king and said, "Let me live in your home. Be patient, I will make your son well again."

Immediately the wise man approached the royal table, stripped off his clothes, and sat down naked next to the prince.

"Who are you and what are you?" demanded the king's son.

"I am a turkey like yourself," the wise man replied. "I thought you might be lonely and decided to come and keep you company for a while."

A little time passed and the "turkeys" grew accustomed to each other and soon became good friends. They ate crumbs, drank from tin plates, and discussed the advantages of being domesticated birds rather than men.

One night, when the royal family was having dinner, the wise man signaled to the king, whose servants brought two silk robes and cautiously placed them under the table. The wise man quickly donned a robe and before the prince could say a word said, "There are some turkeys who are so insecure they believe that by putting on a robe they might turn into something else."

The prince thought for a moment, nodded his head, and began to clothe himself.

Some days later the wise man decided to eat beef, potatoes, and fresh vegetables from a plate. He bit into the food and said, "This is delicious. It's good to be able to enjoy all kinds of food." The prince readily agreed and ate his fill.

Finally, after more time passed, the wise man decided to sit at the table. While eating with the royal family, he called down to the prince, "Come and join me. The food is the same but the chairs make a big difference. Besides, we turkeys have a lot to offer. Why should we remain hidden?"

The prince came out and sat at the table. It was only a matter of time until he remembered who he was.

—*Rabbi Nachman of Bratzlav*

Don't Worry About the Consequences of Your Actions

When I say *Just do it,* I'm reminding you not to dwell upon the *consequences* of your actions. Forget about the outcome. Just focus on the action itself. The wise man simply made friends with the prince. Don't give a gift to someone with the secret expectation of a thank-you, a gift, or a favor in return. That is not "just doing it"—it's living from an ulterior motive. Acting with an ulterior motive always produces lack of balance, because half of your attention is on what you're getting back in return. And when you don't get it, you become angry and resentful. Your gift was not a true gift. It was a form of manipulation.

Don't go on a date and sit there wondering if you're making a good impression and saying all the right things. Just be there with the other person—truly be there. Focus your attention on him, make friends, really listen, really answer. Enjoy the time for what it is, and find out about the person without expecting anything in return.

Expectations generate fears of being disappointed. You monitor your behavior so you'll get what you want. When you monitor your natural behavior, you automatically become split. Half of you is always checking on how the other half is doing—if you're getting what you want. You are not truly there for others. Instead, you are using the other person as an object. You can become an object to yourself as well, pushing yourself around. It's even possible to become frightened of yourself.

STOP and pay complete attention to where you are, whom you're with, and what is actually going on. Be fully available to whatever is happening in your world.

If you are alone, listen to what you hear, see what you see, feel the breeze on your face, notice your posture and how your body feels. Right at this moment, what are you doing? Put your full attention on that. If you are chopping vegetables for soup, pay attention to each chop. Notice what happens to your anxiety now.

If you're focusing on results, then anxiety, fear, and dread appear. If you just throw yourself completely into the action, enjoying and doing it fully, you receive satisfaction in the doing, and fear vanishes. This kind of focused, wholehearted, single-minded action is a wonderful medicine for fear of all kinds. It is also called mindful living, or being present for whatever comes along.

No target is erected
No bow is drawn
The arrow leaves the string.
It may not hit,
But it cannot miss.

—*Zen saying*

Discover Your Life Purpose

When life seems flat and meaningless, fantasies can provide energy and excitement, and it is easy to become addicted to them. Some of these fantasies can make you feel as though you've found your life purpose. Sooner or later, however, that feeling will subside. If your true purpose is not found in fantasy, you might wonder where you can find it and how to get in touch with that which is truly meaningful to you.

STOP and see which of your fantasies have worn out. Are you still clinging to them? Are you reaching for new ones? Can you stop all of that for a moment, let the fantasies go, and simply live in the space that has been created by having nothing, at the moment, to hold on to?

When your fantasies wear out, instead of taking time to experience your life without them, it's easy to reach for new ones. It can seem scary to live in the emptiness, the unknown space that appears initially, between one way of life and the next. However, as the Lankavatara Sutra tell us, "When you give up what is false, that which is true comes all by itself." When you give up your fantasies, your true purpose will naturally be revealed. As you inhabit this seemingly empty space in your life, you will discover that it is actually a treasure-house, full of all kinds of new possibilities.

The great Zen master Dogen tells us: "If fish are taken out of water, they will not live. Water is life for fish, air is life for birds."

What is life for you? What is it that provides you with true sustenance and nourishment? When you find that, you will become deeply at home in the world and not get lost in mirages, lose your bearings, or be run by fear.

MAKE A LIST of the fantasies that you cling to. Now give up one for a few days. See how it feels. What comes to replace it? Perhaps you'll give up hoping that a long-lost lover will suddenly return. What is it like to realize that the relationship is over? How does your life feel without him? What new action can you take now? What is really needed?

There is tremendous power and release of anxiety when you allow yourself to be with the truth of your situation and permit what happens next *to be revealed*. Instead of trying to control reality, you are there, full of interest and curiosity, allowing things to take their course.

Allow It to Be Revealed

Heaven is acceptance of what is.

—*Lubavitcher Rebbe*

Allow is a beautiful word that naturally runs counter to *fear*. As you allow what is real and nourishing to become revealed, you stop interfering with life, people, events, and yourself. You are not demanding an outcome or interfering with the flow of events. If a choice or decision is needed, you don't tie yourself into a knot to make it happen, but allow it to be revealed. Living in this manner, enormous relief and energy become available. Too often, your energy is spent pushing, demanding, and driving everyone crazy trying to figure out answers to the problems you face. As soon as a challenge appears, you jump on it, start to think, plan, strategize, agonize, and place yourself in a prison without bars. Most of these problems, however, aren't even real problems—just other forms of fantasy.

ALLOW yourself something easy: Allow the light to come up in the morning or the sun to set at night. Now allow something else to happen that might be more difficult to accept. Allow your partner to speak as much as he wants and allow yourself to listen, without saying a word.

By allowing life to be what it is, you are saying no to anxiety and control. Allow high tide to be high and low tide to be low. Trust that there is a direction, a life force, a source of guidance that knows what is right in each moment. Stop struggling, straining, demanding, and plotting. Ease up and *allow* this source of wisdom into your life. It knows what is real, what is good, what is true for you. It's with you at every moment. You have just not yet *allowed* it to be revealed. Now is the time to practice *allowing,* another strong medicine in dissolving fear.

There was once a lonely young woman who longed desperately for love. One day, while walking in the woods, she found two starving songbirds. She took them and put them in a small, gilded cage and nurtured them. The birds grew strong and greeted her every morning with marvelous songs. She felt great love for the birds and wanted their singing to last forever.

One day, the girl left the door to the cage open and the larger bird flew out. She watched anxiously as he circled high above her, and she was so frightened that he would fly away and she'd never see him again that when he flew close, she grasped at him wildly. She caught him in her fist and clutched him tightly in her hand. Suddenly she felt the bird go limp; she opened her hand and stared in horror at the dead bird.

Then she noticed the other bird hovering near the door of the cage and could feel his great need for freedom. She lifted him from the cage and tossed him softly into the air, then watched as he circled, once, twice, three times.

As the girl continued to watch, her delight in the bird's enjoyment of his new freedom was so great that she no longer cared about her loss. Just then, the bird flew closer, landed softly on her shoulder, and sang the sweetest melody she had ever heard.

Letting go and letting life take its course is also an act of love. The more you let go and trust life, the more life brings beautiful gifts to you. And your own intuitive knowing develops and guides you to what is truly meaningful and dependable, releasing a great deal of imbalance and fear.

Welcome Intuitive Knowing: Dialogue with the Voices Within

We are all part human, part turkey: We want to hold on to strange images of ourselves and let go of others. There are many different voices that live within each of us. In order to get in touch with your own intuitive knowing, you must become aware of and listen to the voices in you. These internal voices, however, often have conflicting needs and send different messages that can cause you to lose your bearings and sabotage yourself.

You may choose to take a course of action, for example, and in the middle of your journey an inner voice tells you to turn 180 degrees. You start a new project, and suddenly another voice assails you with doubt and fear. Or perhaps you fall in love and are happy, until a different voice begins to point out only the negative things about the other person. Which voice is real? Which is true? Which one can you depend on?

You seldom ask these questions because more often than not you aren't aware of the different voices that are speaking from within, sending conflicting messages. Instead, you just run here and there, reacting to random impulses. In fact, these impulses are not random, but are direct responses to the different voices within.

Although some of your inner voices may generate fear, it's extremely important to learn how to listen to them. Because these voices can be threatening, you tune them out, thinking you do not hear what they say. In fact you do hear, though unconsciously. Subliminally, your inner voices affect your behavior and feelings. Blocking them out becomes dangerous, because you lose clarity and the power to make positive choices for yourself.

Just becoming aware of your many inner voices is tremendously liberating. As you allow them to speak, and as you turn within and listen, not only do your confusion and fear subside, but you find that there is much valuable information waiting to be heard. When a part of yourself operates in silence, unheard, unaccepted, and unknown, confusion develops. But when that voice is allowed to speak out, when you listen, accept, and thank it, a lot of your energy becomes freed up. Shame also dissolves as you make friends with and integrate all the different aspects of yourself. (For an exercise that helps with this process, see page 180.)

Developing Intuitive Knowing

> If you accept the world,
> The Tao will be inside you
> And you will return to your primal self.
>
> —*Lao-tzu*

Within you—indeed, within each of us—there is an original, primal self who can handle anything.

This wiser, primal self is your own intuitive knowing, eternal wisdom, or the master within. *Ask* what it would like to be called, and allow it to run the show. This part of you is grounded in the truth of your being and knows what it is doing and where you need to go.

The practice of dialoguing with your inner selves is very powerful. It's so easy to give your attention to others and to external demands and then wonder why you feel so empty, deprived, or alone. When you give time and loving care to yourself, the little child within who longs for attention feels as though someone is finally there. Other parts of yourself that have been hidden crave expression and acceptance as well. When you stop and listen respectfully to what's going on inside, give every inner voice a chance to be heard, you become more alive, free up your energy, and reclaim the fullness of who you are.

As you do this process repeatedly, you learn to give yourself what you have always longed for from someone else. Now you don't have to cook up fantasies, dreams, and mirages to fulfill your desire to be cared for and understood. You will actually have what you need.

TURNING POINT

There Are No Mistakes, There's Only What Happens

There are many reasons why you may escape from reality into fantasy, including fear of being wrong, shamed, or making a mistake. To call something a mistake, however, is only putting a label on it. In reality, there are no mistakes; there's only what you do, and then what happens. If you view what happens one way, you can consider it a great success. If you view it another, you decide you have failed and disempower yourself.

You must take action in order to grow, explore, and enjoy life. It is better to fall down and get up again than to become stuck and frozen, or to retreat into dreams and mirages. And remember, each time you fall down and get up, each time you take a risk, you have won; you have weakened fear's grip on you.

FOUR

PRINCIPLE 4
Finding a Safe Harbor

Pain and the effort to be separate from it are the same thing.

FOR MANY OF US, LIFE IS A DANGEROUS JOURNEY, where no one comes out alive. None of us gets out unscathed, either. As we move along, we accumulate many wounds and scars. For some, the entire purpose of the journey becomes to keep safe from harm and avoid as much pain as possible.

If you live this way, however, you shut out many possibilities, and will seldom taste the most wonderful aspects of your time here on earth. Living defensively, you are no longer available for connection, creativity, adventure, and the precious experience of love. To experience all of that, you have to become open, vulnerable, and willing to experience a certain amount of hurt and pain.

The Dangerous Journey

There are many ways in which you may experience harm, and some are more manageable than others. Some kinds of harm are impersonal: The economy shifts, suddenly wiping out investments or savings; you become the victim of a flood, war, earthquake, or fire. In these cases, it seems as though larger forces of life are acting upon you, and you have little personal control.

Nasrudin was riding along one day when his donkey took fright at something in its path and started to bolt.

As Nasrudin sped past some countrymen at this unexpected rate, they called out to him.

"Slow down, Nasrudin. Where are you going, riding so fast?"

"Don't ask me," shouted Nasrudin wildly, "ask my donkey."

—*Indries Shah*

In order to gain control and be protected from harm—to prevent your donkeys from running your life—you might prepare for danger ahead of time, buying insurance, finding a safe place to live, hiring financial advisers, undertaking preventive medical treatments, and building up your physical well-being. Or you may turn to religion, pray for the blessing of protection, and seek to live an upright life. None of this is ill advised, of course: It is simply the fear behind these protections that can become crippling in other ways.

TAKE A MOMENT and notice the ways in which you prepare for danger or for anything else that might be unsettling in your life. What is it you are most worried about?

You can experience the pain and harm of life in many ways. You may well see it as the result of impersonal forces, like storms, epidemics, or economic downturns. Other times the harm can feel directed at you personally. You may lose your job, receive a physical injury, or experience some kind of physical attack. Your possessions may be stolen; someone may break into your home. The intensity of fear that arises in these situations is usually acute and difficult to shake.

Your peace of mind can also be stolen—although it may not be obvious when it's happening, and you may not be aware of the consequences. For example, many of the conversations we engage in daily steal our equilibrium and peace of mind.

Martha overheard negative comments being made about her by her co-workers. She wasn't exactly sure what they were saying, however, because they became very quiet when she walked by. This allowed her imagination to run wild and caused her to

feel anxious and alone. Then, in turn, Martha began speaking
about those co-workers to others. Before long she found herself
caught in a vicious cycle of suspicion and ill will.

There are conversational terrorists out there, just waiting to fill you with gossip, rumors, fear, and dread. If you do not know what's happening, you may not realize that you're being harmed, you may have no defenses against it, or you may be unable to make it stop. At this point, a general sense of anxiety arises, and you often end up handling it in dysfunctional ways.

Even your personal relationships with people you trust and hold dear can become unpredictable. A crisis may arise when a friend says something cruel or you become the butt of a joke or an insult. In the midst of a wonderful relationship, a jealous person can intrude and attempt to destroy the connection. This kind of personal, emotional pain can be harder to bear than physical suffering.

WHAT ARE SOME OF THE WAYS that you handle emotional pain? Do they work, or is there a greater price you may be paying for them?

Most of us do not know how to deal with painful emotions and instead turn to drink, drugs, and diversions of all kinds to put an end to them. But these ways of resisting pain cause more fear and pain in the long run. The question really becomes how you handle stress, how you can enter relationships and not end up wounded. In order to do that, you have to find a safe harbor from the storm, where you can live undisturbed and not be tossed around by fear and pain.

Understanding and Handling Pain

In order to find true freedom from pain, there is a fundamental assumption that must be questioned. It is the idea that pain is terrible and must be avoided at all costs. Usually, as soon as you start to feel pain, you immediately try to make it go away. You'll do anything to find a way to change, soothe, or suppress what you're going through. But if you stop, even for a little while, it's easy to see that lasting comfort doesn't come that way.

At the very beginning of my Zen practice, during a retreat in the middle of winter, I was sitting in the back part of a Zendo (a place where Zen meditation is practiced) that was adjacent to a beautiful Japanese garden. The entire Zendo was unheated and, because no one is permitted to move during Zazen meditation, except for brief meditative walks between each sitting, I became incredibly cold after practicing for hours. No matter how many sweaters I piled on, I could not get warm. To top it off, a senior student walked over grandly at one point and flung the door to the back garden open, intensifying the atmosphere and allowing an icy wind to blow in. It was too much. Sitting there shivering, I was furious.

Finally, it was my turn to have *dokusan*, an interview with the master. This was the first one I'd ever had. When the bell rang, announcing that he was ready, I ran up the stairs to the room he sat in.

The Zen master sat there, unshakable, as I sat down in front of him.

He nodded. "How are you?"

"Freezing!" I shouted.

"Then freeze!" he shouted back and immediately rang his bell, to announce that the interview was done.

When you're freezing, freeze. Freeze thoroughly. Nothing more needs to be said. Instead of guarding against pain and running in the opposite direction, stop and allow yourself to feel what you are feeling. Feel it thoroughly. Not only feel it, welcome it. Whatever the discomfort is, it comes with a gift in its hands.

The master gives herself up to whatever the moment brings.

—*Lao-tzu*

After the meeting with the master, rather than doing as he suggested, freezing thoroughly, I spent a lot of time indulging in the flotsam and jetsam of personal reactions: *I must have done something wrong*, I thought. *He probably can't stand me. No, there's something wrong with him. What kind of place is this where they open the door in the middle of winter and let the freezing-cold air blow in?* On and on and on. By looking for all kinds of explanations, I became more distressed. The other alternative was that I could have simply stayed fully in the moment, experienced what was happening completely, and let it be what it was.

Pulling Out the Poison Arrow

> *It is not the answer that enlightens, but the question.*
>
> —*Eugene Ionesco*

The Buddha has said that all life is suffering. This statement has been thought to be pessimistic. The opposite is true. The statement does not suggest that you should fear life, shut down, or refuse your experience. What the Buddha was saying is that suffering is inevitable. By learning how to interact with it wisely, you have the possibility of ending your suffering once and for all. The Buddha said that he was a doctor who had come to cure the ills of the world. The reason there was so much suffering was that the world had been shot with a poison arrow, and he had come to pull this poison arrow out. What is this poison arrow? How do you pull it out and become safe from harm?

The poison arrow is your own reactions to events. It is not necessarily the event that causes the pain, but the way you react to it. How you respond is a choice you make. Once you make that choice, you are starting to pull the poison arrow out.

Taking Charge of Your Responses

There was once a man who scratched himself. His scratching became so bad that people kept asking him why he did it.

All he could say was, "I don't know."

That answer wasn't acceptable. A solution had to be found. Physicians were called in, but after many tests none could find the source of the scratching. There were all kinds of secret theories about it. Perhaps he had done something evil and was now being repaid (bad karma ripening). Or perhaps he had a dreaded disease that could spread to others if not looked after. Perhaps he should be avoided?

Many offered elaborate explanations that could not be proved. Others provided esoteric conjectures. A few sought metaphysical causes. Nothing helped.

Finally a wise old healer came to town. The man who was still scratching sought him out, begging to know the reason. "Why am I scratching?" he asked.

The wise healer thought about it. Then he said, "I have applied my intellect to the problem and I can give you the answer now. You are scratching because you itch."

—*Indries Shah*

The definition of *responsibility* is "the ability to respond." Many of us do not yet have that ability—we just *react*. We itch and itch and create all kinds of explanations for the itch, which only makes it worse.

When you just react, you are easily affected by everything—events, people, and your interpretations of what's going on. You become like a puppet, flailing in the wind. Someone says something nasty and you become filled with hurt; someone else says something seductive and you fall under the spell. Reactions are automatic, are impulsive, and seldom bring wisdom or healing in their wake. Responses are different.

TAKE A LOOK at some of your automatic, knee-jerk reactions. What is it that usually gets a reaction from you, where you don't have much control? When you are at the mercy of everything that's happening, it is so much easier to be played with and harmed.

In your search for safety and freedom from pain, it's easy to spend a huge amount of time and energy trying to change people or situations. That's a waste of time. More often than not you can't change what is happening in the moment, but you can take charge of your reactions and learn instead how to *respond*. This is tremendously important, because once again it is not people or situations that are producing fear and pain, but your *reactions* to them. This cannot be emphasized often enough.

As you become aware of your negative reactions and dissolve them, you are no longer at the mercy of conditions and individuals. You can go where you like and be at ease with whatever happens, and whoever is there. How you *respond* is in your hands.

Turning Upset into Peace of Mind

Perception is not neutral. As you perceive, so you are. And as you perceive others, so they are to you. Your perception of a situation will elicit different responses from you, as well.

To help you see the ways in which you usually react to situations that are upsetting, and explore some alternative ways to perceive them, take a look at the following scenarios. As you reperceive each of them, you will have a different response that will turn what would usually be an upset into peace of mind:

- **YOU WANT SOMETHING AND CANNOT HAVE IT**

  Rather than feel deprived or punished, you could take a larger view and see that perhaps whatever you desire may not ultimately be for your highest good. Perhaps there is more to learn from *not* having it. Focus on the ways in which *not* having your desire causes you to grow. Focus on what you *have* been given and appreciate it with a full heart. What happens to your feelings of deprivation now?

- **YOU HAVE SOMETHING AND FEAR LOSING IT**

  When the time comes for things to change, when you have to let go of something that's important to you, it's natural to suffer the pain of loss and react with grief, fear, or bitterness. You might not even allow yourself to have something important again, for fear of losing it.

  How else could you respond? You could focus upon what you have received and see it as a *gift*, not something that belonged to you in the first place. You could be grateful for the time it was yours and think of ways of offering this gift to others. Stop and see what benefits you received from it. What did you learn? How are you different because of having had it? Why not then share the joy and wisdom you received with those who need these?

When something is taken away, most people feel as if they must fight to hold on, or to recapture that which they have lost. If this is your response, what you are failing to realize is that, when it is time for something to go, no matter how hard you fight for it, if the time has passed, if it is not yours, it cannot stay. In fact, although you do not realize it, it is usually in your best interest for it to go. It makes room for something new in your life. By letting go graciously, you will be able to savor the lessons and joy you had from the *gift* and grow as a result of the experience, rather than fall apart.

• YOU HEAR A NEGATIVE COMMENT ABOUT YOURSELF
You may be inclined to either defend yourself or attack when others say negative things about you. You might also actually start to believe the bad things that have been said about you, take them in, and start to punish yourself by becoming self-destructive.

Instead, realize that people rarely attack others unless they are hurting and in pain themselves. The person who has attacked you is expressing his own fear and pain. You do not have to accept this person's hurtful comments as the truth. Refuse to take in the other person's poison, and stay planted in truth of who you are. You do not have to be dependent upon others for your sense of self-worth.

• YOU CAN'T GET ENOUGH OF WHAT YOU WANT
You may find that no matter what you are given, you always want more. In the very midst of receiving, you feel it is not enough, are unable to be satisfied. This insatiable hunger is called the pain of greed. The more greed you have, the more deprived and empty you feel, and the more frightened you are that you'll never feel full.

Instead, you could learn to fully taste, digest, and enjoy whatever is given to you, become able to absorb its nourishment, and discard the waste. You could become willing to simply experience your hunger, right down to its very core. Even though this is a difficult concept to accept in the present "super-sized" culture, where more is always good and less is always bad, it is important to do so. You only crave more because you are unable to fully experience what you have. When you actually taste and are grateful for what you have, you feel full and complete.

If you can, focus upon being grateful, even for a little bit. You can then go a step farther and remind yourself that your hunger will never be fulfilled by simply taking more and more. A wonderful teaching from the Tibetan Buddhist Lojong tradition addresses this: Whatever you receive, simply say, "This suffices."

• YOU LONG FOR CONDITIONS TO BE DIFFERENT

Most of us long for conditions to be different. In the midst of illness, for example, you may long for health. Somehow you are not able to accept each moment just as it is. You feel you must change life—overpower it with all your ideas about how everything should turn out for *You*. This self-preoccupation may be called the pain of arrogance, the idea that everything revolves around your personal needs, and that the whole world exists to suit *You*.

To escape from the anger and fear that this generates, realize that others are just as important as you. Reach out to make life better for them as well. Understand that conditions change constantly. Rather than fighting, hating, and resisting a difficult condition, welcome it as a teacher. This acceptance brings forth new, constructive responses and—best of all—brings peace of mind.

• WHEN PAIN COMES FOR NO KNOWN REASON

The worst kind of pain comes for no apparent reason, with no explanation of where it comes from or what it means. All of us require meaning; we need to grasp why something is happening. Suffering that comes for no apparent reason can be called the pain of meaninglessness. When you are faced with this kind of despair, you can become nihilistic, feeling that nothing ultimately matters. Or you might lose interest in living and loving, and retreat into a shell.

A different way of responding to the pain of meaninglessness is to realize that it has come into your life so that you can face and look more deeply into the true significance of your time here on Earth.

All pain and suffering arise to demand that you pay attention. You may have been pushing yourself too much, living foolishly for too long. *Stop and listen,* the pain is saying; it is asking you to take a good look at what's going on. Chances are you have never learned to stop and pay attention, respect what you're feeling, give it time and space in your life. When you begin to do this, however, your pain does not turn into suffering. You are pulling the poison arrow out.

STOP AND ASK YOUR PAIN the fundamental questions: "Why are you here now? What do you want from me? What is it I have to learn?"

When Medicine Turns to Poison

Most of the time we do not know the difference between medicine and poison, between what is beneficial and what is toxic in our lives. What tastes sweet might be poison; what tastes bitter could be good medicine. You may love a food, person, or situation that is harmful, perhaps because you are addicted or think something good will finally come of the relationship.

Or you may be in a relationship that tastes sweet and might not notice the ways in which it weakens and undermines your life. On the other hand, a person, job, or situation may taste bitter, be difficult initially, yet be beneficial in all kinds of ways. Struggling with a difficult person or circumstances can strengthen you, allow you to tap into your courage and strength. You may think you are up against danger and harm, but the situation may be a gift in disguise.

Most of the time, however, we decide what is good or bad based on whether we like it or not, whether something tastes bitter or sweet. But this is a limited perspective. There is a wonderful Zen koan that explores this conundrum: "The whole world is medicine. What is the illness?"

This saying asks you to look more deeply at what is truly beneficial in your life, and what really causes distress or harm. It doesn't say directly what the illness is; it just asks you to look. It also suggests that when you look only for sweetness, when you avoid bitterness or pain, you are strengthening the illness, increasing fear in your life. When you are willing to engage with all of your experience, to taste the bitter and the sweet, you are taking a medicine that ultimately makes you stronger. How much power can fear have in your life when you are willing to accept your pain? When you are willing to take whatever comes, fear no longer can keep you living a small, secluded, shut-down life.

————

We eliminate the doctor by accepting the disease.

—*Henry Miller*

————

Medicine turns to poison, and poison can turn to medicine as well. Tony Papa, an artist activist and author of *Fifteen to Life,* tells a wonderful story of how what started as a nightmare turned into a transformational experience in his life.

> I was in my late twenties with a wife and child when I desperately needed some extra money. Things were tough. It was my kid's birthday and I wanted to get him something special. For a small amount of extra cash, a friend gave me a package to take to someone else. I didn't know what was in it or the guy I took it to. It was a drug bust. The cops grabbed me on the spot and although I had no previous record, I was given a sentence of fifteen years.
>
> Horrified, my life destroyed, locked up in prison, I was desperate. There seemed to be no way out. In the beginning I cursed at everything and hated life. I was miserable all the time. Then, after about a year, something amazing happened. I found a way out. Even though I was still imprisoned, I became a free man. I got interested in painting. I started to paint, loved it, couldn't get enough, couldn't stop. I spent every spare moment in my cell painting, and then began to study all other painters' work. I could feel something inside me changing. Before long my work was being sent out to others to see. I was included in exhibits. People were responding. They loved my work. It was exciting. Life was good.
>
> My paintings began to not only to be included in shows all over, but accepted in the Whitney Museum. As I became well known I

realized I could use this to help others, became a spokesman for unfair drug laws. I started to do that. I also taught other inmates painting, studied law, and when I was finally released after twelve years, set up a foundation called Drug Policy Alliance, devoted to repealing extreme drug laws and helping others in this situation find a way out. I call myself an artist activist now and a communication specialist for Drug Policy Alliance.

When I was put into jail I thought my life was over, but it was there my life really began again. When I stopped hating and fighting everything, the situation became my ticket to real freedom. And not just for myself either. The pain I went through was a good thing in the long run.

Tony's jail cell became his road to a new life, filled with creativity and wisdom, where he learned to become a force for the good.

Pain Is Not Suffering

Pain is not suffering. It is just pain. You cut your finger and it throbs. You become ill and your body aches. A dear friend dies and you mourn. These are natural life circumstances that cannot be avoided. They are not to be feared, but taken for what they are. Realize that pain is just pain. It does not mean you will feel this way forever, that you are being punished, or that the rest of the world is about to fall apart. Pain is just an experience you are having, and if you do not resist it, it will leave naturally, making room for whatever comes next. Experiences come and go, like clouds in the sky. When you do not resist or hold on to them, they float away on their own.

It is so tempting, however, to turn pain into suffering, which is harder to cope with. At the beginning of Tony Papa's incarceration, when he hated and fought everything that was going on, he suffered greatly. When he accepted the situation for what it was, he began to find ways to grow inside it. His cell turned into an art studio, his imprisonment turned into a journey toward a life of real worth.

The way we turn pain into suffering is to dwell upon our pain and make it mean something terrible—blame others for it, talk about it to everyone, use it to get sympathy and attention. You may feel you are being singled out for unfair treatment, or become a victim or martyr. When you engage in this kind of behavior, suffering becomes a way of life. This kind of suffering can become addictive.

HOW DO YOU turn your own pain into suffering? What causes you the greatest suffering in your life now? Are there benefits to your pain? What are you getting out of it? What would happen if it were gone?

Some people actually seek pain. For them, suffering has secondary benefits. Masochists and martyrs, for example, love their pain, hunger for it. For them, suffering provides an identity, a way of interacting with the world. It can also provide a justification for expressing anger or getting revenge. These individuals enjoy making others feel sorry for them and guilty about their pain. It's a grand manipulation, as if they're saying, *Look how much I'm suffering, now you have to do what I want. How can you add to the pain I'm living in?*

Others feel that due to their suffering, they can act any way they like, be as nasty as they want, demand anything. Some crave suffering because they feel guilty and seek punishment to assuage their guilt. These individuals attract, seek, and cling to suffering.

When pain turns to suffering, it can easily become a lethal force. A life lived in suffering is a life based on fear. You fear being happy, successful, or loved. You fear working through problems and letting conflict subside. You can be in a wonderful relationship, which you inevitably sabotage because you cannot allow yourself to have happiness or fulfillment. That would mean letting go of your suffering. Who would you be without your suffering? How would you interact with the world?

> *John had a pattern of being with a woman for about six months. The initial stages of the relationships were wonderful, but as feelings deepened, and the women wanted more, he began to find fault with them. Not one of them fit the bill. There was no reason to continue the charade. Before long, he was alone again. After each of the relationships ended, he blamed the women, but he also missed them, and did not understand what caused this pattern.*

One day John realized, "I just couldn't take being so happy. It didn't fit my picture of myself. I didn't know who I was when I was happy. I needed something to complain about, someone to fight."

John's sense of self disappeared when things were going well. Therefore, he held on to an identity fueled by suffering and fear. John was addicted to suffering.

ASK YOURSELF, who would you be without your suffering? What would you talk about with your friends? How would you make others care for you? Where would you get excitement from in life?

False Expectations

It is as if we change the very course of life by changing our attitudes towards it.

—*Henry Miller*

A great source of fuel for our pain and suffering is the false expectations that run our lives. Like John, we all live with a blueprint of expectations of how things should work out. These expectations direct the ways in which we relate to one another and even our sense of self-worth. Most of the time these expectations are simply illusions, with no basis in reality. Yet when life does not live up to what we're expecting, not only do we feel fear, but we also expend every effort to make reality fit with our demands. It can be painful to look at our expectations and put the false ones down.

Mulla Nasrudin is a wonderful classic character in Sufi teachings: the wise fool who always seems to make mistakes, do the unexpected, and not understand what is going on. In his disconnection from conventional understanding, a deeper, spontaneous wisdom manifests.

Some small boys planned to steal Nasrudin's slippers and run away with them. They called to him and pointed to a tree. "Nobody can climb that tree," they said.

"Any one of you could," said Nasrudin, "and I will show you how."

He removed his slippers, then tucked them into his belt and began to climb.

"Nasrudin," they cried, "you won't need your slippers in a tree."

"Why not?" Nasrudin said. "Be prepared for every emergency, I say. For all I know I might find a road up there."

—*Indries Shah*

Reality is reality. It takes place as it wills. It's clear that on a literal level Nasrudin will not find a road up in a tree, even if he expects it could happen. (This story has deeper implications, however, about finding your road, or pathway in life, in unexpected places.) Yet the larger point is that reality is not your enemy, but it certainly can become the enemy of your expectations. You start a business and expect it to succeed in a year or two, you choose a life partner and expect to be happy the rest of your life, you enter a race and are sure you are going to win. You are trained to see all of life through the lens of your expectations. You are even told that certain people are good, and others are bad—and you expect it to be true.

Needless to say, reality often brings experiences that contradict these deeply held beliefs. Each time this happens, fear develops. What is important to see is that it is not reality but your *expectations* that are causing the trouble.

WHEN YOU ALLOW REALITY TO BE REALITY, YOU
GROW SAFE AND STRONG.

MAKE A LIST of your basic expectations of life. How do you expect others to treat you? How do you expect to perform in work, in love, in life? Are there some expectations that do not serve you? Which ones can you give up?

This is a fascinating exercise. As you do it, you will see how rigid some of your expectations can be. Expectations do not factor in change, growth, or new developments. They do not allow you to see that life constantly metamorphoses in front of your eyes. What was medicine one day turns into poison the next, and what was poison turns into medicine. Someone who was angry becomes forgiving. Someone who forgave you can develop a grudge. Someone who loved spending time in the sun grows older and now seeks the shade of trees. Expect life to be life, expect everything to alter, and then you will be safe and secure in the ever-flowing panorama of change. As you release yourself from false expectations, you can enjoy and relate constructively to whatever life brings.

LIST five expectations you can easily let go of. What is it like to live without them? Where is the pain now?

Letting go of expectations does not mean you let go of your standards, values, or boundaries. It simply means that you develop the flexibility to take appropriate actions and make choices that are constructive. When you cling to false expectations, you get tied up in anger, struggle, and heartache, sometimes rejecting those you care for the most. These expectations are a suit of armor that does not really protect you, but just provides another way of becoming numb.

> One of the boys at Nasrudin's school asked: "Which was the greatest achievement, that of the man who conquered an empire, the man who could have but did not, or the man who prevented another from doing so?"
> "I don't know about any of that," said Nasrudin, "but I do know a more difficult task than any of those."
> "What is it?"
> "Trying to teach you to see things as they really are."
> —*Indries Shah*

Craving Excitement and Challenges

> *There are two tragedies in life. One is not to get your heart's desire. The other is to get it.*
> —*George Bernard Shaw*

On the one hand, we all want to be safe. On the other, we crave excitement, challenges, and danger.

If you don't have something to overcome, an enemy to conquer, someone to captivate, an obstacle at work, competition in sports, your life can seem pointless. Indeed, challenges are one way in which you test your mettle and grow. You set a deadline; accept a difficult assignment at school, at work, in sports, or on the battlefield. You climb high mountains, dive deep into the sea, fall in love with someone who is unattainable. You try to conquer other countries or convert people to your beliefs. There are many ways in which you seek excitement and challenge, which often provide a sense of meaning and purpose in life.

Challenges have many different purposes and outcomes. Sometimes they are dangerous and damaging; while at other times they provide a way to stretch and touch something noble and courageous within yourself. In fact, the more fearless you become, the more life-giving challenges are brought to you, and the more you enjoy them and grow strong.

Life itself brings all kinds of tests and challenges. There are challenges that can be constructive: a scientist in a laboratory challenging himself to overcome a dreaded illness, an athlete attempting to win a world record, a young mother challenged to care for a child well, despite endless demands. You are suddenly called upon to take an action that makes you larger than you knew you were. You may have to jump into the ocean to save someone who is drowning, or run into a burning house. You may be presented with a lost orphan whom you decide to take into your home.

It is very important to distinguish between healthy, life-giving, constructive challenges and those that arise from attachment to danger, suffering, and harm. Some challenges tear you down, creating obsession, misery, and inevitable failure. Others help you grow upright and strong.

Constructive Versus Destructive Challenges

TAKE A LOOK at the main challenges in your life. Which ones have you chosen, and which ones have chosen you? Which ones are stimulating and enjoyable? Which challenges enhance your sense of who you are? Which ones tear you down?

It is very important to distinguish between constructive and destructive challenges. Sometimes you create repetitive challenges that are based on your desire to suffer and live in fear. Other challenges are based on your desire to overcome fear, grow strong and brave, and enjoy life fully. Distinguish between these two kinds of challenges in your life.

DRAW A LINE in the middle of a page and write down the two kinds of challenges on either side. See yourself giving up one of your false, destructive challenges today. Tomorrow give up another one.

The challenges that are positive and healthy for you are part of the journey to becoming fearless. Even though you experience difficulty, pain, or failure along the way, by forging ahead the fear will diminish and you will grow.

The challenges that are repetitive or obsessive, that make you weak, are destructive, counterfeit challenges. They are substitutes for the real thing. These challenges may create a false sense of excitement, but usually they involve a situation where you cannot win, or where someone else will be in pain—gambling with your family's income, for example, being in a volatile relationship, or refusing to seek medical care even though you are ill. These are not the kinds of challenges that produce strength or well being. Instead, they arise from a love of danger, an attachment to suffering, or a desire to receive or inflict harm. See these challenges, this false sense of excitement, for what they are and let them go.

When you begin to let go of false, destructive challenges, at first things may seem empty and dull. You may wonder where the excitement or the purpose of your life has gone. It may be necessary to go through this period of boredom or emptiness in order for true challenges to appear. In fact, you may be holding on to destructive challenges because you have no idea what your true life's challenges are. Addicted to the fear that false excitement generates, you may have blocked out the enormous, beneficial excitement and challenges that life naturally provides. You have not allowed yourself to see the thrill of what is truly waiting for you, or who you can really become.

Answering the Call

The following story from Lakeesha Walrond, executive pastor of the First Corinthian Baptist Church, Manhattan, explains how she took on an incredible challenge and in the process discovered who she truly is:

Due to huge, unexpected changes in my life, I began to go through a period of fear, emotional death, and what felt like suffocation.

At this time God literally picked me up and saved me from sure death. In the midst of this pain, through deep prayers and meditation, I was literally called to go on a forty-day pilgrimage with God.

When I first received the call, I didn't want to leave my family, life, or church. I was afraid to go, afraid to stay, consumed by fear. When I heard God tell me to go, I said, that's not God's voice, though deep down I knew it was.

Then, one day, the call was confirmed by another person. Although I hadn't said anything about this to anyone, a woman at the church, whom I hardly spoke to, came over to me and said, "Why are you still here? God wants you to go."

I was shocked, but her words penetrated my soul and I knew I had to go.

I received details about the trip from God every step of the way. I was told that life was simple and I was to live in the simplicity of life. From the very beginning, there was to be no luxury in this voyage. Travel was to be by bus and train only, so I could take my time and embrace the beauty of Creation. This was daunting, as I had never traveled by bus or train before. I always flew. There was to be no jewelry, nail polish, makeup. I could take only take a few sets of clothes for forty days.

I could only stay in monasteries and convents, to start. I had to completely leave the country. There were four parts of Creation I had to see—these represented the four elements.

The first was Niagara Falls, representing water; the second was Mount Saint Helens, representing wind; the third was the Grand Canyon, representing earth; and the fourth, the Everglades, represented sun or fire.

When I left I took the train up to Niagara Falls and I prayed and said, *God, what am I doing? I've only traveled by myself once before in my thirty-seven years.* When I arrived at the first stop, I called the Catholic church—looked in the Yellow Pages and called the diocese and told them I was on a forty-day journey and needed a place to stay. They responded, "Yes," and gave me some numbers to call. I did the same and stayed in convents in each city I traveled to.

It was very simple there. There was no luxury, no phones, television, entertainment, or distractions. All of the places had at least one worship service a day; some had four. The cost was minimal and included meals. One of the places kept silence; in the others you could talk.

In Canada I connected with a woman at the convent who was on her own personal retreat. She wanted to take me to a garden. In the garden we decided to pray under a tree. As we were about to pray, a man came up to us from out of nowhere and said, "Do you know this tree?"

We looked at him a bit strangely and said, "No."

"This is the European linden tree. It is a very famous tree in my country and is different from the American linden." Then he pulled a leaf off and gave it to each of us. He showed us the back of the leaf, which had hairs, and said this was the only way we could tell the difference between the European and American one. He continued, "This tree is in front of all the churches in my country, and there is one in front of my house. Years ago, there was a bad storm and a huge branch broke off the tree, and it began to corrode and rot. But over the next thirty years the tree grew another branch in the same place. Trees don't do that. But this tree has the ability to heal itself."

We were speechless, teary-eyed, and I knew in my own spirit that God was saying to me, *Like this tree, I've given you the ability to heal yourself because I am within you.*

And we prayed. It was beautiful.

When I was alone with God's Creation it was so beautiful and awe inspiring, I recognized how much of the little things about Creation I had learned to ignore through the busyness of my life.

For example, just taking the time to look at the sky and to fully appreciate the birds and trees. The amazing thing was that all the while, I'd been living in a place that was full of life, trees were growing, grass was growing, birds were singing, squirrels were dancing. There was life all around, but I was dying. How could I be dying in a place where there was so much life?

By stepping outside my personal situation, I was able to reflect and see the truth of it. Through this journey I learned to conquer my fear by embracing and understanding that life is difficult and challenging, but there is beauty in the difficulties because it makes us stronger. I learned to really embrace the inconsistencies of life as a gift.

At the end of the journey I came home to a life in which the circumstances had not changed much, the challenges were still there, but I was no longer afraid. I was in a place where I could embrace life.

Through this experience God birthed in me a new ministry, Total Refuge. This is a nonprofit organization that is geared to help women and teenagers to overcome the wounds of sexual abuse. And in this way, the fear and pain I suffered became the fertilizer for a new life and new hope for many.

TURNING POINT

Let Reality Be Reality

Reality always brings what is needed, whether you like it or not. The more you welcome what is being brought to you—feel it, taste it, know it—the more you release false expectations and are able to learn the lessons you need to learn. Then you can open your treasure-house, access your enormous inner resources, and receive the plentiful nourishment and support that are waiting for you.

FIVE

PRINCIPLE 5

Blessing Others: Deeds of Love

Let your fellow's honor be as dear to you as your own and do not anger easily.
—YOCHANAN BEN ZAKKAI,
FIRST-CENTURY JEWISH SAGE

SELF-HATRED IS ONE OF THE MAIN illnesses in the world today. When this illness strikes, it often manifests as depression, which is anger turned against the self. It arises when you have not have not been given permission by yourself or anyone else to express yourself constructively. Repressed anger festers within and finally turns against you, as you punish yourself in all kinds of ways. Although this may not be done consciously, it happens nevertheless.

People who are in the grip of self-hatred have a negative and fragile sense of themselves. They crave respect and approval, and often choose socially acceptable partners, jobs, and lifestyles. In this way, they feel as though they are respectable and fit in. However, when their cover is threatened and their vulnerabilities and problems come to light, not only does self-hatred emerge, but hatred of others comes out as well.

A Zen student came to Bankei and complained: "Master I have an ungovernable temper, it causes me to hate both myself and others. How can I cure it?"

"You have something very strange," replied Bankei. "Let me see what you have."

"Just now I cannot show it to you," replied the student.

"When can you show it to me?" asked Bankei.

"It arises unexpectedly," replied the student.

"Then," concluded Bankei, "it must not be your own true nature. If it were, you could show it to me at any time."

—*Zen story*

The Malevolent Mind

The malevolent mind is fueled by the poison of anger. It is unable to stop for a moment and take note of what it is feeling or how it behaves. It is a mind that has lost perspective. Once it takes over, there is no end to the damage it creates. In some cases, it becomes focused on revenge; at other times, on dominating and getting its way.

When you feel threatened, attacked, or not properly valued, the malevolent mind tells you that attacking in return will make you safe or restore your wounded pride. But it doesn't—the opposite is true. Attacking in return makes you more fearful of repercussions and takes your self-respect away. Hatred is no respecter of persons. Much like in an autoimmune disease, where the body attacks its own organs, hatred eats up your well-being. If you are in the grip of the malevolent mind, you can easily become prey to alcohol or drugs and spin out of control, even suffering serious health conditions such as heart attack, stroke, and physical symptoms of all kinds.

When the malevolent mind becomes unstoppable, it crushes whatever stands in its way. In many respects, it is like a wild animal on a feeding frenzy, not caring who the victim is. In its grip, you can harm those who are closest to you, especially yourself. Of course there are different degrees of malevolence, and times when you can see the light and be reasoned with. Other times you cannot.

————

Who is wise?

He who knows the consequences of his actions.

—Pirkei Avot

(*The Wisdom of the Fathers*)

————

Action taken as a result of anger is often thought to be an expression of strength. The sense of power you feel when attacking makes it seem as if what you are doing is undeniably right. However, after the hatred passes, and you've left things worse than they were before, you usually feel weak and depleted. The rush that comes from anger is a substitute for real strength. Real strength requires that you have the ability to refuse the urging of the malevolent mind, have the clarity to see the situation in its largest perspective, and be able to respond compassionately.

In this day and age, we see the proliferation of hatred and violence being acted out all over the world and in many of our lives. In order to get rid of this poison, it is not sufficient to deal with the branches (expressions of anger); we must go to the roots and pull them out.

Uprooting the Malevolent Mind

> With gentleness overcome anger
> With generosity overcome meanness
> With truth overcome deceit.
>
> —*Buddha*

The Manataka American Indian Council preserves and protects the culture of the American Indians. The following story is a classic tale told many times during ceremonies around the sacred fire.

A grandson came to an old grandfather. The boy was filled with anger and told a story about a friend who had done him an injustice.

The grandfather said, "Let me tell you a story. I, too, at times have felt great hatred for those who have taken so much, and who feel no remorse for what they do. But hate wears you down and does not hurt your enemy. It's like taking poison and wishing your enemy would die.

"I have struggled with these feelings many times. It is as though there are two wolves inside me. One is good and does no harm. He lives in harmony with those around him and does not take offense. He will only fight when it is right to do so, and in the right way. But the other wolf, ah! The littlest thing will send him into a fit of temper. He fights everyone, all the time, for no reason. He cannot think because his anger and hatred are so great. It is helpless anger, for it will change nothing.

"Sometimes it is hard to live with these two wolves inside me, for both of them try to dominate my spirit."

The boy looked intently into his grandfather's eyes and asked, "Which one wins, Grandfather?"

The grandfather smiled and said quietly, "The one I feed."

Even though you may not be aware of it, the malevolent mind has many ways of taking root and growing in your life. One powerful way is for it to tell you that you are right and others wrong, life is a battle and you have to win, others are your enemies, it does not matter whom you crush on your way to the top of the ladder. The malevolent mind tells you that if someone hurts you, you must hurt him back, twice as hard, to prevent this attack from ever repeating. The malevolent mind simply does not realize that any action taken in hatred does not stop the situation from happening; in fact, it ensures that it will.

You cannot find peace through attack. The more hatred you send to others, the more it returns to your own life. This is a basic law of life. It is irrefutable and constant. Those harmed will rise up, sooner or later, and get their revenge. If they do not do it personally, you will draw some other angry person or negative situation back to you. These are the cycles of karma, destiny, and sorrow. How to put an end to them?

STOP for a moment and see what it is that causes hatred in you. What do you do when it takes hold? How do you prevent it from digging in?

In order to dissolve fear, you have to work with the hatred in your own life. Because this feeling is so unacceptable to most of us and to society at large, usually anger and hatred go underground. You repress your hatred, smile nicely, and do all you can to act as though you are so spiritual or holy that anger never approaches you. However, anger approaches all of us. The malevolent mind is always there, waiting for an opportunity to flare up. In order to truly root it out of your life, you must first be willing to face it and acknowledge it for what it is.

When you do, a funny thing happens. Like fear, as soon as you look it in the eye, expose its lies, anger begins to wobble and fade away. It has no power on its own, just what you give it. When you believe the lies it tells, it metastasizes like cancer. However, when you are on the alert and say no, you are in effect pulling out the roots. The many ways of saying no to anger fill you with the vitamins and minerals of the soul. They build up your spiritual immune system and make you strong.

Pulling Out the Roots of Anger

Different roots feed anger and hatred. Once you realize what they are, you can begin to pull them out.

> *No matter what Vinny did wrong, he could not see it. It was everyone else's fault. He was right and they were wrong. He had a thousand and one excuses for whatever he did, and always felt others were the villains. Needless to say, this not only destroyed his personal relationships, but took a huge toll on his life at well. He could never say he was sorry or correct his errors responsibly.*

Stop Justifying Anger

One root of anger is the ongoing justification of it. Some people feel that it is natural, even healthy to be angry and to take it out on others. (It's one thing to express anger in a healthy, responsible, constructive manner, and quite another to use it to attack, blame others, condemn, deceive, and so on.) When you're involved in justifying your anger, you can find all kinds of theories, beliefs, and reasons to allow anger to rule your life.

Like most of us, you've also been taught to believe that if people offend or insult you, it is healthy to let them have a piece of your mind. If you don't, you'll become a doormat. Some people are always looking for insults and slights from others,—just waiting for an opportunity to let their anger out.

WHAT DO YOU DO when you feel sideswiped, insulted, offended? How do you handle your anger? Do you lash out or pretend it hasn't happened? Do you return insults and go on the attack? Or do you take responsibility for your response and communicate your feelings clearly?

Responding to Insults

There are many ways of responding to insults constructively that keep you from getting sucked into a negative whirl. In fact, you can even approach the experience of being insulted as an opportunity to grow. But first you have to believe that being insulted can have a positive outcome. The insult may have come to you to clear karma—to balance something negative you might have done in the past. Or it may have come to help you build strength and endurance, to teach you not to respond impulsively. Perhaps you are being invited to develop compassion, to look more deeply at who the other person really is.

If you do not take the insult personally, it cannot hurt you at all. Realize that the person who insulted you had to be in pain to behave in that way. The insult simply shows you that he or she is in need of compassion and care. You could respond with kindness; you could offer understanding in return.

Here is an example from Zen stories about the samurai. It shows a different way of handling anger that arises.

> There was once a great warrior and though he was still quite old, he was able to defeat any challenger. His reputation extended far and wide, and many students came to study with him.
>
> One day, an infamous young warrior arrived. He was determined to be the first one to defeat the great master. Along with his strength, he had an uncanny ability to spot and exploit any weakness in an opponent. He would wait for his opponent to make the first move, thus revealing a weakness, and then would strike mercilessly with great speed. No one had ever lasted beyond the first move in a match with him.
>
> Against the advice of his students, the old master gladly accepted the young warrior's challenge. As the two squared off for battle, the young warrior began to hurl insults at the old master. He threw

dirt in his face. For hours he verbally assaulted him with every curse known to mankind. But the old warrior merely stood there motionless and calm. Finally, the young warrior exhausted himself. Knowing he was defeated, he left, shamed.

Somewhat disappointed that the master had not fought the insolent young man, the students gathered around the old master and questioned him. "How could you endure such an indignity? How did you drive him away?"

"If someone comes to give you a gift and you do not receive it," the Master replied, "to whom does the gift belong?"

The master had conquered his own pride and self-importance and could not, therefore, be thrown off balance and harmed.

Living in a Black-and-White World

Another root of the malevolent mind is the idea that the world is divided into two camps: People are either good or bad. Of course, you are always in the right camp and everyone else in the wrong one. And of course, it's fine to hate those in the wrong camp—even to destroy them. Perhaps you prove your self-worth by declaring others bad or wrong.

False pride keeps you looking down on others, projecting your fears on them, not seeing who they truly are. It prevents you from behaving in ways that would be beneficial to all. When you're in false pride, you do not stop to realize that the person you consider your enemy today may become your dearest friend tomorrow. Friends turn into enemies and enemies into friends all the time. We do not live in a black-and-white world. Change is constant, including a change of heart and mind.

Eating Your Shadow

THAT WHICH YOU CANNOT ACCEPT IN ANOTHER IS SOMETHING YOU CANNOT ACCEPT IN YOURSELF.

Your shadow includes the suppressed, unacceptable aspects of your nature that you have denied and repressed, including attitudes, memories, or desires you cannot face or accept in yourself. It's much easier to see the negativity in others, hate and fight them for it, than to face these qualities in yourself. This shadow has a powerful influence and affects your life in all kinds of ways. Because you have to keep it hidden, it drains energy from you, keeps you in conflict, and makes you generally miserable.

> *Wherever he went, Pete ran into men who were making passes at married women. This agitated him greatly. Pete hated both the men and the women who went along with it. Safely, respectably, and unhappily married, Pete was frustrated and lonely. He was completely out of touch with his own desire to do the same thing. The men who were making passes at married women were showing Pete what he hated and rejected in himself. As soon as he could see and accept these qualities in himself (not necessarily act on them, but own and accept them), not only did his upset diminish, but he stopped attracting these situations in his life.*

Once you face your shadow, your energy and well-being are freed up. Now you don't have to blame others for that which you cannot accept in yourself. This is called eating your shadow. It is such an important concept that it is well worth stopping and really taking it in. If there is someone you hate, reject, feel agitated by, realize that you have attracted this person to you and that he or she is simply showing you something you cannot accept in yourself.

BECOME AWARE of the qualities you hate or find unacceptable in others. Then look and see how these qualities also exist in yourself. Find times when you have behaved or felt just as they do. Decide to accept these qualities in both of you.

The more you repress aspects of yourself and project them onto others, the more you will attract people who mirror them. Worst of all, when you refuse to face the shadow within, when you spend time projecting it on others, paranoia can develop. Then it becomes easy to feel that the entire world is malevolent, plotting harm behind your back. Not only is this a projection of your own hatred, but it can also be an unconscious wish to be harmed.

Nasrudin, the well-known hero of many Sufi stories, shows us over and over the ways in which all of us can be fooled by the world as we know it. In his unexpected ways of thinking and behaving, he points to greater truths.

Nasrudin had words with the head of a monastery where he was staying. One day a bag of rice was missing and the chief ordered everyone to line up in the courtyard. Then he told them that the man who had stolen the rice would have some grains of it in his beard.

This is an old trick, to make the guilty party touch his beard, thought the real thief, and he did not move.

The chief is out to revenge himself upon me, thought Nasrudin, *and he is certain to have planted rice in my beard. I had better brush it off as inconspicuously as possible.*

He clawed his fingers through his beard and found everyone looking at him.

"I knew you would get me sooner or later," said Nasrudin.

Universal Paranoia

Just because I'm paranoid doesn't mean they're not out to get me.

—*Thomas Pynchon*

Paranoia is completely driven by fear. Truly paranoid individuals are totally out of touch with reality, only imagining the worst, seeing danger, hearing a sneer or sensing an attack behind every word spoken to them, and feeling the entire world is out to get them. If someone is just casually grimacing, the paranoids immediately decide that the other person is on the verge of an attack.

Everyone can be subject to paranoid moments, but there is a continuum here. At first, perhaps, the fear may last only for a few moments. But if you are not careful, true paranoia can grow and take over your life. Paranoia is so disabling because it prevents you from seeing clearly, decreases your options, intensifies fear, and peoples your world with enemies. It is crucial that you understand how it operates—both personally and among nations—and how to undo it.

When paranoia strikes, you begin to attribute dark motives and suspicious behavior to others; you become convinced you are confronting dangerous enemies and have to remove them from your life. You do not see the shared humanity between you, only what is different. You do not realize that like you, these individuals want to be happy and avoid sorrow, that like you they have suffered and want to be safe, that one day, like you, they will face death.

When fear is activated, it is very easy for the paranoid mind to flourish. It is also easy to respond in a paranoid manner when confronted with individuals from another race, religion, or culture. Because these people seem different and unfamiliar, it is easy to project the worst upon them. The more you see someone as an enemy, the more you allow the paranoid mind to grow, the more you actually call those qualities out in the person. Perception is fatal. As you see others, so they respond.

What you see in others, you bring out in them.

When you see the worst in people, you send them an unconscious message about who they are to you, and unconsciously they fulfill that role. This dynamic operates on many levels—between parents and children, husband and wives, and friends and lovers, as well as other nations and religions. When an individual, group, or nation is treated with respect, on the other hand, they *sense* it and it affects their *sense* of themselves and how they respond to you.

CONSCIOUSLY FIND the best qualities in someone you think ill of. Dwell upon that. Then find something else you can admire about her. Think of a time she helped you or did something you liked. This will balance out the negativity you see in her and open new possibilities for the relationship.

An ancient Zen story tells us about the famous Master Bankei and his way of dealing with negative behavior:

When Zen Master Bankei held his retreats, students from many parts of Japan attended. During one of these retreats, a student was caught stealing. The matter was reported to Bankei with the request that the culprit be expelled. Bankei ignored the case.

Later, the student was caught in a similar act, and again Bankei disregarded the matter. This angered the other students, who drew up a petition asking for the dismissal of the thief, stating that otherwise they would all leave in a body.

When Bankei read the petition, he called everyone before him.

"You are wise, brothers," he told them. "You know what is right and what is wrong. You may go somewhere else to study if you wish, but this poor student does not even know right from wrong. Who will teach him if I do not? I am going to keep him here even if all the rest of you leave."

A torrent of tears cleansed the face of the student who had stolen. All desire to steal vanished.

Self-Centered Absorption

Self-centered absorption is a stop on the road to paranoia. When you become completely absorbed with yourself, the whole world revolves only around you and you feel grandiose, tremendously important. In this frame of mind, you take everything personally in a self-referential manner. If someone is not giving you the honor and attention you deserve, that person is cast out of your life.

When you are absorbed with yourself, you want the good only for yourself, not for others. You are driven to protect yourself and everything that you identify with. At the same time, you reject others. This is an awful way to go through life. Once again, this is a continuum. It's normal for all of us to have moments like these, but unchecked, the self-centered mind can grow and become your basic way of being in the world.

The self-centered mind operates in bad faith. Other people become objects to be manipulated so they can glorify and serve it. The self-centered mind doesn't see others as equals, sometimes not even as human beings with the same rights, needs, and desires. Others are only there to serve and validate its beliefs.

TAKE NOTE of the ways you are involved in self-centered obsession. To whom do you refuse kindness? Whom do you condemn? What kind of fantasies do you entertain about people who seem quite different from you?

Self-centered absorption does not express the basic truth of who you are. Living a self-centered life, you are simply encasing yourself in a cocoon that creates more of a prison than a safe resting place. In order to dissolve paranoia, you must learn how to unravel the cocoon created by the self-centered mind. At first this can be frightening, because the cocoon feels so familiar and safe. The longer you stay inside it, however, the more you are insulated from the world, and the less you understand and know how to respond to it. This cocoon itself puts you in danger. The safest place is out in the air, under the wide open sky.

HOW DO you cocoon yourself? In what areas of your life are you centered only upon yourself? Where do you curl up and hide?

Releasing Hatred—The Practice of Forgiveness

> *If you want to find peace, do peace.*
> —Rabbi Elazar ben Azaria

Contrary to popular belief hatred is not at all difficult to release. When you are in a dark room, all you need is a little bit of light to make the darkness disappear. The same is true of hatred—all you need is for a little compassion to enter the situation, and the darkness of hatred quickly subsides.

IT'S EASY TO GET RID OF ENEMIES. TAKE THEM TO LUNCH. LET THEM BE THE STARS. THINK OF WAYS YOU CAN GIVE TO THEM. TURN THEM INTO FRIENDS.

There are many different ways of releasing hatred and developing forgiveness, but the first requirement is the willingness to do so. If you don't really want to release your hatred—if you think you need to hold on to it because it serves or protects you—that will be an impediment. (To practice forgiveness, take a look at page 185, in the Workbook section of this book, and try the simple exercises. They're enjoyable and effective.) Each interaction you have with another person presents the possibility of heaven or hell. It's good to be able to choose your own destination and not be ruled by anger and fear, which seem to arise automatically and try to run the show.

Forgiveness does not mean remaining in a toxic or abusive relationship, or participating in something that is harmful for you. It simply means letting go of the anger you feel and wishing the best for the other person. When you do so, you then become able to make healthy choices for yourself.

You can't control the way another behaves, but you *can* control how you choose to respond. Choose love; choose health. Don't choose to be caught in the quagmire of pain. When you are determined to see others only as good or bad, you limit your perception of them and aren't able see them, or yourself, in the largest context possible.

Life is a process of constant flux, in which every person contains everything. Whatever another human being has experienced is also within you. Because the flow of life is constant, you can be very angry one moment, then wake up filled with love the next. There is always the possibility of change, growth, and renewal for everyone. When you see others in that light, you help them grow and you are living a life of forgiveness. You are also removing yourself from the trap of the malevolent mind that keeps you chained to fear.

When you live a life based on forgiveness, you cannot be harmed. And the power that comes to you to be constructive and joyous is enormous. A wonderful example of this is the life of Rabbi Joseph Gelberman.

Rabbi Joseph Gelberman, the original founder of the interfaith movement in the United States, is a wonderful example of a man who has lived his entire life in deep forgiveness. He always greets students and friends with his heart wide open. Ninety-seven years old and going strong, he is completely vital and offers talks, workshops, and holy schmoozes while marrying couples and running his seminars with joy. In many years of knowing him, I have never known him to judge, blame, or speak ill of anyone.

Originally raised in Hungary, Rabbi Gelberman lost his entire family—parents, sisters and brothers, wife and daughter—in the Holocaust. The difference between him and many others who survived, however, was his response to this great nightmare. Rather than allowing himself to become bitter and angry, he said simply, "I will live enough for all of them now." He chose to devote his life to creating dialogue and making peace among the different religions so that hopefully, hopefully, a tragedy like this will never happen again.

His teachings revolve around ways of responding to anger and fear. The song he sings constantly, both out loud and to himself, is simple: "God is with me, I will not fear."

"Fear is only false evidence appearing real," the rabbi often says. "If you truly know that God is there, and that he loves you, how can you fear? You become frightened or upset because you forget. All anxiety, fear, and anger come because we do not know that God is right there.

"Fear is a mistake and also a sin," he says. By sin, he means it is missing the mark. "It's a testimony to the fact that you have forgotten who you are and who is with you every moment.

"I learned a lot from my father," the rabbi tells us. "One time, years ago, back at home in Hungary, our entire family went to the synagogue for the Sabbath, as was our custom. When we came home a robber had broken into our home and had stolen everything. He even took our Sabbath meal. There was nothing left at all. My mother started crying and my brothers and sisters were filled with fear. My father just clapped his hands loudly and said, 'Stop, it's the Sabbath. This robber can take everything from us, but he cannot take our Sabbath joy. He cannot touch our souls.'

"Then he began singing and dancing in honor of the Sabbath, and we all joined in.

"I never forgot that beautiful afternoon. Whenever anything terrible happens, I remember that whatever anyone does, they cannot take my joy from me, they cannot touch my soul, if I do not give it away. That is up to me to protect.

"One of the reasons I've lived so long is that I do not pay much attention to nasty words or angry faces, either. When someone is very unpleasant, I just thank God I'm not like that and don't take it in. It's important to find something beautiful in everyone, and this is what I try to do. Do I love everybody? No, but I don't hate anyone.

"In all of us there are two selves, the *Yetzer Harah* and *Yetzer Hatov*—the evil inclination and the good inclination. When we focus upon building our good inclination, when we focus upon love and acceptance, the evil inclination disappears.

"Another reason I've lived so long is because I discovered the eleventh commandment. That is—'Thou Shall Have Purpose.' You have to know what you're here for, what you have to do.

"I'm tutoring a young man now for his bar mitzvah who, at first, was quite uninterested in the teachings. Finally, one day, I said to him, 'Do you realize that God needs you?' This got his attention. He was surprised. 'He needs you very much,' I told him. 'You're important to him. He can't do everything by himself, alone.'

"The young man was surprised. It made him very happy. He went home after the lesson and told his mother, 'Mom, did you know that God needs me?' The mother smiled. 'What I do is very important,' said the young man.

"After that our studies changed. He hung on every word I said.

"Know your purpose. God needs all of us. Unless we know what we are here to do, it's easy to be filled with fear. Once we know, we have direction, and we have support. Then there's no reason to fear anything. We have God on our side.

"When you have found your purpose, you have found your true partner. Take time to understand this. Take a little walk with God each day, become closer, ask about your purpose, and become quiet, so you can hear what God has to say.

"What you are doing then is building faith. Faith keeps us standing tall no matter what happens. In each of us there is a candle, but in some it is not yet lit. Time alone with God helps us light our candle so we can see where we're going, and also give light to others who have gotten lost on the way. Our job is to keep this candle burning. And how do we do so? Basically, it's quite easy. At graduation of my seminary, all my students sing the same song. They sing one phrase over and over. This is a song designed to light their candle and keep it going strong.

I am ready, I am ready, I am ready
To do the good and the beautiful.

"You can sing this song, too, whoever and wherever you are. Then do more than sing the song—start to do what it says. Find something that is good and beautiful and do it every day. When you are busy doing that, fear will never have a hold on you."

Developing Self-Respect

We become sick because we act in sickening ways.

—Louis Jourard

Like Rabbi Gelberman, the outgrowth of a life of forgiveness and goodwill is self-respect. It is impossible to be filled with hatred when you live a life based on respect. The illness of self-hatred is a direct consequence of a lack of respect, both for yourself and the world you live in. To dissolve self-hatred, simply look and see if you are living a life worthy of respect.

Living a Life Worthy of Respect
Deep within each of us there is a strong sense of what is meaningful, what we value and respect. Some are in touch with this, others not. Whether you realize it or not, however, your inner self reacts negatively whenever you act against your true values and that which has real meaning for you. The price you pay for this is lack of self-respect.

On the road to becoming fearless, it is essential to get in touch with your innate sense of what you truly value. When you sell out, when you violate your inner trust, you become easy prey for self-hatred. An excellent antidote to this is living a life you can respect.

STOP AND TAKE NOTE of the people you respect most in life. Who are your heroes and heroines? What have they done in your eyes to deserve your respect?

This will show you what you value most. Then look and see if this is present in your life right now. If not, include it. Fill your life with self-respect.

When you truly respect yourself, you cannot disrespect another. You automatically see what is valuable in others and respond in a positive manner. As you do so, you begin to live a life worthy of respect.

Repairing Lack of Self-Respect

We've all made mistakes, some more serious than others. But all of your own mistakes can be repaired when you're not mired in self-hatred. Self-hatred keeps all wounds alive and makes you feel guilty much of the time. You may think that by feeling guilty, you're doing something worthwhile, repairing what you've done wrong. But in fact, you're not. Guilt, a substitute for true reparations, is toxic in many ways. It often prevents you from taking the actions that would correct the situation and allow you to move forward.

TAKE A LOOK at what you've done that you're feeling guilty about. Now ask yourself what you need to do to repair this situation. Is an apology needed? Is there a service you can offer? If the person you've wronged is gone, can you make it up by offering something to someone else? Only you know what is truly needed.

See what is needed and do it today. The actions you take will be deeds of love and respect—respect for yourself and the world you live in. These deeds turn mistakes into growth and benefit everyone. Because it is impossible not to make mistakes, the real question is: Have you done what is needed to repair them? Have you turned your errors into beneficial actions or a foundation for a life worth living?

Begin right now to see what is needed and repair one error at a time. (See page 187 in the Workshop section of the book for more detailed directions.)

Deeds of Love and Blessings

A feeling that's here one minute and gone the next cannot be considered love.

—*Kabir*

Deeds of love heal wounds and prevent fear from arising. But first it is important to understand what love is. Love is not necessarily a feeling. Love is a verb, an action you can take no matter how you are feeling. Feelings are like the weather: They come and go. Although you are not in control of your feelings, you are always in control of how you behave. You can always offer deeds of love. There are many actions you can take that become blessings to you and the entire world.

When you offer deeds of love, you are receiving protection against the effects of anger. When thoughts of anger or hatred arise, immediately replace them with a deed of love. As you bless others in this way, you are blessed as well. And as you do this, you will see your life expand and prosper. No deed of love offered goes unappreciated, no matter whom you offer it to.

Danny, who lived in Brooklyn, was up at Fort Tryon Park, near the Cloisters, in Manhattan. A dog that was skin and bones came over and put his head right on Danny's lap. A friend of Danny's friend who was with him at the time asked, "What should we do?"

Danny said, "I'll take him back home."

She said, "But how? We don't have a car and it's a long subway ride and you're not allowed to take a dog on subway."

Danny then went and borrowed a belt from someone he knew in the neighborhood to make a leash for the dog, and took him on the subway. No one stopped him, and there was no trouble during the hour-and-a-half ride. The dog obeyed and sat at Danny's feet.

Danny then took the animal to his small house to feed and bathe him. At night the dog howled like a coyote, disturbing the neighbors, who complained. Danny shifted the dog to the basement of his home and padded the windows so there wouldn't be any noise. After two weeks of eating well and enjoying Danny's backyard every afternoon, the dog looked sleek and his coat was shiny. Then one day, the animal ran away.

Danny looked for him everywhere and missed him greatly. He often wondered how he was. Then one afternoon, while sitting outdoors on the stoop, Danny noticed a pack of stray dogs coming down the block. In front of them was the dog he'd cared for. Danny was thrilled to see him. The dog stopped at the stoop, didn't move, and gave Danny a long look. Danny felt good. He felt the dog had returned to thank him, before he rejoined the pack to move on.

Discovering Your Deeds of Love

> *Happiness comes from being loving, not from being loved.*
>
> —*Erich Fromm*

It's easy to find out what your deeds of love are. For each person it's different. Take some time and make a list of deeds that are meaningful to you. What makes you feel cherished and loved? Which deeds express your love for others? Some people need to receive gifts, cards, flowers, while others feel cared for when a friend promptly returns a phone call or shows up on time. For others, it is very important that their friends keep their word. Any breach of trust makes them feel unloved.

Think of some actions you take that express your concern and love. Again, this differs from person to person. Some examples might be cooking a meal for someone, visiting a friend in the hospital, or running errands for a neighbor who needs the help. Take the time to find out both how you enjoy giving to others and what others actually need. It's important to ask others how you could be of service and find out what matters to them.

Compare the deeds of love on your list with the deeds you do each day. There may be a large discrepancy. Take some of the deeds of love on your list and include them in your daily living. No matter what mood you're in, do at least one a day. It's especially good to do these deeds for those you're having difficulty with. By thinking of them kindly, by extending yourself, not only will you wipe out your own negativity, but you will learn to see these other people in a totally new way.

Blessing Others

AS YOU BLESS OTHERS, SO ARE YOU BLESSED.

You have the power to offer blessings, which means to encourage, enhance, and uplift all of life. The words you speak to others can be powerful forces for good. When you do not take charge of your words, when you speak negatively to someone, rather than lifting them up, you are tearing them down. Your intentions have a strong impact on your relationships and the outcome of your activities. By offering a blessing, you are sending a deep intention and wish for a person, activity, or project to flourish.

Whenever you become aware of having a negative thought about someone, stop and bless the person instead. Say, "I send you a blessing that all the goodness you desire comes into your life. I bless you for health and well-being."

You can bless and enhance activities and projects as well. When you offer the work you do a blessing, or bless a project you or someone else is involved in, you are taking time to send powerful, loving energy to it. As you regularly practice offering blessings to others and to yourself, you will be amazed at how your health, well-being, and joy in life will be enhanced.

Looking Through the Eyes of Love

> Through love, all that is bitter becomes sweet
> Through love, all dregs turns into the purest wine.
>
> —*Rumi*

What follows is a process that takes only a moment or two, and quickly turns upsets into happiness:

FOR A MOMENT, think of someone you know who doesn't much like you. Look at yourself through that person's eyes. How does it feel? Probably not so good.

Now think of someone who really loves you, thinks the world of you. Look at yourself through this other person's eyes. How does that feel? Probably wonderful.

It's so easy to turn things around. Are you willing to keep looking at others through the eyes of love, and keep looking at yourself that way, too? You never have to succumb to self-hatred or hatred of others. It only takes a moment to change your point of view.

TURNING POINT

Even a Little Bit of Love Dissolves All Kinds of Hatred and Pain

Even a little bit of love is atomic. It has the power to cause incredible changes in our minds, bodies, and hearts. We all have the power to extend love and offer blessings. We all have a great deal of love within us. As you choose love rather than hatred, not only do you heal your life, but you heal the entire world.

---

112 | *Fearless*

PRINCIPLE 6

Letting Go of Control and Domination

Do you think you can take over the universe
And improve it?
I do not believe it can be done.
The universe is sacred
You cannot improve it,
If you try to change it, you will ruin it.
It you try to hold it, you will lose it.
—LAO-TZU

THE NEED TO BE IN CONTROL OF ourselves and our environment is fundamental. The entire universe, and all that lives in it, is an ecosystem, with a natural balance and equilibrium. Storms, earthquakes, forest fires, and other disruptions ultimately take place in order to restore natural balance. Even death makes way for change, so that new life can grow. When it is not interfered with, nature constantly replenishes itself. There is an ultimate harmony and wisdom that prevails.

Human beings, however, seem to have an innate fear of losing control. Many people share the illusion that their world and relationships will fall apart if they do not exert control. A great deal of life energy is spent constantly trying to control. Being out of control is equated with going crazy, losing your mind and yourself. Being out of control can also be likened to the eruption of intense desire that cannot be fulfilled or the presence of emotions that cannot be integrated. In fact, all humans are filled with incredible energy—with emotions, desires, dreams, and abilities that are largely kept repressed and "under control."

It is well worth understanding the different aspects of control. There is healthy control, the natural, harmonious control of nature, where things work together effortlessly and the body and mind are in balance, functioning optimally. With healthy control, you do not constantly focus on whether or not your liver, kidneys, or marriage is functioning properly. You go about your business, with ease and peace of mind.

Unhealthy control is different. It is generated by fear and is intensified by the rational mind under stress. When something arises that threatens equilibrium, the desire to control takes hold. It is one thing to be in control and another to want control, to feel as though you lack it and are out of control. Oddly enough, the more you try to impose control, the more out of control you become.

WHAT IS IT you feel you need to control? How do you do it? When do you do it? Does this bring ease or security, or do you have to control even more the next time the situation arises?

The Desire to Control: Possessing Others

> Drinking a cup of green tea
> I stopped the war.
>
> —*Zen poem*

All compulsions are fueled by the craving to control. You can feel compelled to control relationships, money, time, work, food, sexuality, feelings, thoughts, behavior. When a compulsion takes over, it's hard to sit down and enjoy life as it is. It's hard to appreciate each moment, to fully taste a delicious cup of green tea.

In the beginning of her relationships, Julia enjoyed being with men who were controlling. It made the man seem strong, and she felt protected. The more possessive a man became, the more she felt he cared for her. However, as his demands intensified and he curtailed her freedom more and more, she felt less and less loved. Soon she began to feel frightened and struggled to get free and find her own footing.

In all relationships, sooner or later, your authentic needs will emerge and demand expression. The more you try to control a relationship, the sooner it will fall apart. No one can be controlled or dominated indefinitely. And, on the other hand, if you allow someone to control you, sooner or later the person controlling you will lose interest in you and stop respecting you. Their controlling behavior may have seemed to be an expression of caring, but it never was. It may simply have been the thrill of conquest.

The Compulsion to Control Relationships

> He inspired others, not by force or domination,
> But by being true.
>
> —Buddha

Control is a big issue in many relationships. Initially, the person who is in control can seem authoritative and powerful, but this is simply not so. Controlling people are actually out of control and can't face or handle their own feelings. They compensate for this by trying to dominate whomever they can. Although dominating others might give them a temporary feeling of strength, when they lose control of the person or relationship, it's easy to see who they really are.

There are many reasons why you might feel the need to control. Understanding what these are can help you step back and let go. When you let go, fear dissolves, you gain your balance, and life begins to flow. At this time, it's easy to see that control ultimately suffocates and has nothing to do with love or goodwill. Trying to control only creates more tension and keeps a larger harmony from prevailing. Practice this and see for yourself:

STEP BACK A MOMENT and stop trying to control. Take a deep breath. Open your hands, open your mind, step aside, and let go. At first you may feel as if this is dangerous. It is not. As you do it over and over, you will see that letting go of control is where your true safety comes from. (See page 188 for other exercises that will help let go of control.)

Dominate or Be Dominated

Sometimes the need to control arises from the fear of being controlled. You may be afraid of being taken over or dominated by someone else, not know how to set boundaries, or feel you don't have the right to say no. It's easy to compensate for this by taking over and dominating. Instead, learn to set healthy boundaries. Give yourself the right to say a guiltless no.

It is important to be aware of your particular patterns. You may try to be in control by allowing your partner to control you, acquiescing to whatever he or she wants. However, as you do this, not only are you strengthening the compulsion to control in the other person, you are wiping yourself out. Your own feelings, needs, and values go unattended. Sooner or later, your resentment bursts out.

Don't allow anyone to control you. See where you really stand, what's important, and hold your ground. If someone leaves you because of this, let them go. This was not a true friend or a healthy relationship in which you could grow.

The urge to control intensifies in romantic relationships, where deep feelings make everyone vulnerable. When you feel vulnerable, it's tempting to compulsively withdraw, sabotage the relationship, or allow suspicion to rule the day. This insidious process can start slowly: Perhaps you need to know everything your partner is doing, whom she's spoken to, where she's gone. Then you may start checking e-mail or phone records. When your partner is out of sight, suspicious fantasies fill your mind. You want to control her actions, choices, friends, family; what she eats and what she wears.

At this point, you may feel your love has grown deeper. However, this is not a sign of love—it's the compulsion to control. Beware: It is harmful and dangerous. Instead of indulging in suspicious fantasies, confront your fears directly. Communicate openly and honestly with your partner. Ask questions, express your needs and feelings, and find out what you need in order to be able to trust. Ask your partner for what you need. Don't imagine she knows what it is, or that if she loved you she would know automatically. Most of the time your partner hasn't the vaguest idea of what's going on inside you. It's very important to actually ask.

Max didn't believe his fiancée, whatever she said,. He knew more was going on. He felt she'd become interested in other men and that she was now giving him all kinds of excuses for what he considered her unsettling behavior. First she started dressing more provocatively, then she wore more makeup and perfume. When he asked her why, she said it was because she wanted to please him. Once again, he felt she was lying. It tormented him and soon he listened to her phone calls secretly, checked her appointments, and even had her followed. Although he found not so much as one piece of evidence that she was lying, he continued to accuse her. The relationship became abusive and, although she loved him, she finally decided to end it. His unhealthy need to control drove her away.

The Gift of Trust

It's difficult to put an end to control if you cannot trust. Trust comes with trusting yourself and being trustworthy. It also comes as a result of time spent with a person, during which you experience who the person truly is. Trust is precious and must be nurtured and protected. If something happens that shakes your trust, attend to it immediately. Talk it over. Get it cleared up. Let your partner know what you need in order to feel trusting, and make sure you're heard. Trust is built through daily actions.

Sometimes your partner can't give what you specifically need in order to feel secure. It may not be something your partner is capable of. This must be respected, and, no matter how much you care, you must also respect the fact that this may not be a relationship where you can trust or that is healthy for you.

When distrust and fear intensify, abuse isn't far away. Some people become nasty in order to keep their partner off balance and afraid. They do everything in their power to criticize and destroy their partner's self-esteem. Deep down they feel that a partner who is really insecure won't be able to leave or find someone else. And in many cases, this is so. The partner just becomes more dependent and takes more abuse.

Why would people behave this way? Because in a distorted way, they feel that by exerting control they are warding off pain. They do not see that they are actually bringing about the painful consequences they fear. If a relationship is to be sustained, the needs of both partners must be honored and attended to. Mutual respect, open communication, and basic trust are essential. Of course it is impossible for all this to happen when either partner is in the grip of the compulsion to control.

————

To give your sheep or cow a large, spacious meadow is the way to control him.

—*Suzuki Roshi*

————

When you allow your partner to be who he is and allow events to take place naturally, you become centered and clear, and it's easy to see what's happening and know what to do. If your partner wants to go, you let him. If he is yours, he will return to you. If he isn't, you can't keep him anyway.

TAKE A LOOK at your relationships. When do you feel out of control, and how do you handle this? Also take a look and see if you might be in a relationship with someone who is controlling you. Make sure you clearly see the price you pay for allowing it to go on.

Now just take a deep breath, and let go of the wish to control.

Healthy and Unhealthy Control

Open your hands if you want to be held.

—*Rumi*

There are healthy as well as unhealthy forms of control. In order to have healthy control in your life, you must tolerate being out of control or balance at times. It is said that an airplane pilot flying to a destination is off target about 99 percent of the time. He is constantly adjusting the route of the plane, taking all sorts of flying conditions into account—wind, rain, altitude, turbulence. The pilot is not caught in the compulsion to control the flight. If he were, he would not have the flexibility and clarity to be able to adjust to inevitable changes in conditions as his journey progresses. He could not land the plane safely.

When the pilot is truly centered and clear, he is present to what is going on, he knows what is needed and is in healthy control.

The same is true of your life and relationships. Caught in the compulsion to control, you lose touch with the natural give and take of daily life, changing conditions, your partner's responses, and what is truly needed from you. This is also true of your relationship with yourself. When you are constantly monitoring and controlling yourself, forcing yourself to live by a set of prescriptions, always having to perform in a certain way, you lose trust in yourself. Rather than honoring your natural rhythms, you are creating a life without balance.

A man found the cocoon of a butterfly. One day a small opening appeared; he sat and watched the butterfly for several hours as it struggled to force its body through the little hole. Then it seemed to stop making any progress. It appeared as if it had gotten as far as it could and could go no farther.

Then the man decided to help the butterfly, so he took a pair of scissors and snipped off the remaining bit of the cocoon. The butterfly then emerged easily. But it had a swollen body and small, shriveled wings.

The man continued to watch the butterfly because he expected that, at any moment, the wings would enlarge and expand to be able to support the body, which would contract in time. Neither happened! In fact, the butterfly spent the rest of its life crawling around with a swollen body and shriveled wings. It never was able to fly.

What the man, in his kindness and haste, did not understand was that the restricting cocoon and the struggle required for the butterfly to get through the tiny opening were nature's way of forcing fluid from the body of the butterfly into its wings so that it would be ready for flight once it achieved its freedom from the cocoon.

—*Afterhours Inspirational Stories*

It's so important to trust natural rhythms. Sometimes struggles are exactly what you need. If nature allowed you to go through life without any obstacles, you would not develop strength; like the butterfly, you could become physically challenged and unable to fly.

Relationships, including the one you have with yourself, are a dance, requiring flexibility, awareness, and the willingness not to be ruled by preconceived ideas or the need for approval or control. The people who are able to receive the deepest, most beautiful experiences in relationships are those who have learned the great art of trusting and letting go.

WHAT KIND OF RELATIONSHIP do you have with yourself? Do you trust yourself to live naturally? Do you allow yourself to deal with obstacles in your own time, or do you impose rigid expectations and demands upon every moment of your life? You can also have an abusive relationship with yourself.

Be yourself, that is all that you can be. Anything else is to go astray.

—*Bhagwan Shree Rajneesh*

Manipulation and Control: Authority Figures

Some of the most lethal forms of control are the ones you are unaware of. These can have an even stronger effect by entering your unconscious mind and acting upon you subliminally, causing you to feel uneasy or frightened without knowing why. Some threat or manipulation has entered your being unknowingly. When you are feeling frightened and acquiescent, it is easier to be controlled in ways that are harmful. Once you have awareness, however, you have the ability to *discern* and can *choose* whether or not you wish to accept the negative suggestion, whether it comes from ordinary people or powerful authorities.

Sue Matthews is a wonderful example of a woman who would not succumb to authority in the fight for her daughter Taylor Matthews's life. Sue refused to accept at face value what anyone told her. She researched her daughter's condition intensively and challenged all assumptions. She was present for every medical procedure and did not go along with established protocol automatically, but constantly sought explanations and understanding. This took daring and courage on her part, but her daughter's life was at stake. In my interview with her, Sue herself described one particular incident that exemplified the struggle she went through.

Once again we could see the blaring red lights of the ER as we quickly passed into the triage room. My daughter Taylor was quickly assessed and set up with IV antibiotics while I conferred with the ER doctors. Because they did not know Taylor's full history and were extremely busy, their answers were usually incomplete and incorrect. As always, I insisted on having them page the on-call doctor, and, as usual, they refused, claiming they could handle it.

But this time I knew we were in real trouble and this was going to be a tough battle.

I paged the on-call doctor myself, pretending I was at home. When I received the return call, I found out the doctor was only a few floors above me in the hospital. I sighed a huge sigh of relief when I knew who the doctor was, and that she would tell me the truth. She came to the ER and confirmed my fears. Yes, once again, Taylor was in a life-threatening situation. Yes, my suspicions were correct, the hospital we were in, the one we were mainly treated at, was not willing to perform the procedures necessary to save Taylor's life. Her lungs had to be drained of fluid, but due to complications and liabilities, they would not do it. They were only willing to give her IV antibiotics.

As odd as this may sound, I was relieved that at least the doctor told me the truth. At least now I knew what I had to do. I didn't have very many choices. My choices were to pull out her IV myself after the antibiotics were complete and try to just walk quietly out of the ER without being noticed, or to tell them I was leaving, at which point I knew they would tell me I could not take her. I walked the halls, noticing that there was not enough activity going on that night to sneak her out.

Oh, why can't I just this time convince them that if we don't leave, Taylor could die? I thought over and over. Then I started my crusade. I started by speaking in a gentle, motherly tone with the least experienced person I could find. Slam dunk, the answer came immediately. It was the answer I was ready for.

"Mrs. Matthews, if you try to take your daughter out of this hospital while she is in a life-threatening situation, she will stay and we will handcuff you, take you to the station, and charge you."

I knew not to fight back. Instead I had to mobilize. I went straight to the bathroom and set it up as my office. My first call was to my husband at home. Desperate, as I was, he immediately started to network with other doctors and hospitals, while I did the same. We checked in with each other every few minutes. Minutes turned to hours, while the two of us kept trying to make other arrangements. In between, I kept checking on Taylor. She was sleeping, and all night long there were new bags of IV fluid, IV antibiotics.

"Hang on, sweetheart," I kept whispering, "you're gonna make it. Daddy and I will keep you safe."

Finally, in the very early-morning hours, I woke Taylor to the brilliance of bright red blaring lights. We had legally escaped; an ambulance had come for us. We were going to be transported to another hospital that was ready to perform the necessary procedures to save Taylor's life.

Different thoughts ran through my mind, including words I once read in a book by Dr. Bernard Siegel. He said that the patient who questions the doctors, who doesn't accept their answers at face value, is the patient with the best prognosis. I had to take the situation in my own hands. Every extra day she got to live was precious. I didn't want her to miss out on any one of them.

Attachment to Authority Figures

Attachment to any system, or person, is a
suggestion of an anxious escape from life.

—*Henry Miller*

Some of us need to have all kinds of authority figures in our lives. It gives us a sense of safety, as if there is someone, somewhere, who knows what is ultimately good and right. That person knows which direction we should take—the right medicine, the best way to live, whom to marry, whom to reject.

All of us have a deep, innate longing for heroes and heroines, a craving to respect, admire, and look up to someone. This is the way a child views his parents. It would be frightening for a child to go through life without parents to look up to, idealize, and rely on for safety. As we grow older, this need should subside. Very often, it does not. Not too many of us are able to mature fully and see others for who they are—individuals with both strengths and weaknesses, struggling to get through their day.

When admiration for another person is healthy, that person becomes an inspiration or role model. When admiration is unhealthy, however, there is a great price to pay. When you put another on a pedestal, you simultaneously disenfranchise yourself. Excessive admiration creates dependency on that person, and you begin to believe that as long as this person is in the world you are safe—that *they* will look after you. It's even possible to make a tacit assumption that this person is closer to God than you. Authority figures relieve you of responsibility for treading this earth with your own two feet and finding your own unique answers and your own unique way.

THERE IS NO BIGGER MISTAKE YOU CAN MAKE THAN TO RELINQUISH YOUR RIGHT TO MAKE MISTAKES.

The more you cling to authorities, the more you open yourself to disappointment when you ultimately see who they truly are. When you realize that your idol is human, can be wrong, confused, manipulative, or even hungry for power over you, this can rock your entire world. Some people are so devastated they can't move on. Others become furious with authority figures and waste years hating them and trying to expose the fraud.

When asked why they committed horrifying acts, many people have said in their own defense, "I was just following orders." Their highest value was to blindly trust and follow what the authorities told them, even if they knew it was wrong and unjust. These individuals disconnected from their own humanity and innate sense of right and wrong. They relinquished their own inner authority, tied themselves up in golden chains, and wondered how they'd gotten trapped.

Not too many people are able or willing to find their own path and walk it, to become their own authorities. Nyogen Senzaki, a wonderful teacher, tells us how:

> "DON'T PUT A HEAD ON YOUR HEAD. WHAT'S WRONG WITH YOUR OWN HEAD ANYWAY?"

WHO ARE THE AUTHORITIES IN YOUR LIFE AND WHY? What is it about them that made you put them in this position? What do they have that you lack? Are you willing to claim those qualities in yourself? What do you have that they might lack as well?

The Sufi sage Nasrudin saw through all forms of authority and the question of right and wrong:

> Nasrudin was made a magistrate. During his first case, the plaintiff argued so persuasively that Nasrudin exclaimed, "I believe that you are right."
>
> The clerk of the court begged Nasrudin to restrain himself, for the defendant had not yet been heard. Nasrudin was the ultimate authority in the situation and had to be fair.
>
> Nasrudin then listened to the defendant and was so carried away by his eloquence that he cried out as soon as he had finished presenting his evidence, "I believe you are right."
>
> The clerk of court could not allow this.
>
> "Your Honor, they cannot both be right," the clerk said.
>
> "I believe you are right," said Nasrudin.
>
> —Indries Shah

It's fine to admire other human beings, to be instructed, inspired, guided, or cared for by them. It's necessary to work in a respectful and harmonious way with individuals at your place of employment who are in authority positions over you. But it is quite a different matter to give another person authority over your inner life, control over your thoughts, choices, decisions, and actions. To do so is to abandon yourself, to pull the ground out from beneath your own feet and wonder why you are so wobbly. And, in fact, you are doing something even more lethal than that: You are inviting this person to manipulate you and hold your well-being in his or her hands. If you are in thrall to a so-called authority, it's time to turn things around. Take back your own power and wisdom. Become fearless. Validate what you know and who you are.

WHERE DO YOU PUT YOUR TRUST? To whom or what do you turn in times of need? Who—or what—never lets you down? Do you know how to turn within yourself? When something happens that you would normally turn to another for, turn to yourself. Sit down and ask yourself what you need, then wait for an answer. The more you do this, the more confidence you will develop in the deep guidance that resides within.

The greatest gift you can receive is to be put in touch with your own enormous gifts and resources. Anyone who wants to take those gifts away, who wants you to turn to them as authority, is not your friend. Why would you throw away your enormous wisdom? Why wouldn't you want to claim it for yourself?

In society, the virtue in most request is conformity. Self-reliance is its aversion. It loves not realities, but names and customs. The only right is what is after my constitution; the only wrong, what is against it.
We are not leaning willows, we can and must detach ourselves. With the exercise of self-trust, new powers appear.

—*Ralph Waldo Emerson*

Religious and Spiritual Abuse
Religious and spiritual practice is an area where authorities dominate, and where fear, control, and manipulation can run wild. True religious

and spiritual practice is so central to life that the abuse of power must be addressed clearly.

Many religious systems are filled not only with authority figures, but also authoritative texts that may not be questioned. If anyone does, the punishments can be severe. Fear runs wild here—not only fear of the issues being explored, but fear of the consequences of not offering unconditional obedience.

When we come to religious or spiritual practice, we come with deep needs and questions that are essential to our lives. We come for ways to understand the enormous mystery of life, and the endless challenges we face each day. Human beings need meaning; we cannot thrive without it. All religious and spiritual practices provide a way through the maze of confusion and despair. This is a crucial journey that we all must take, to connect with that which is greater than ourselves and be released from the grip of fear.

Because this journey is so important, it can be usurped by authorities, distorted by fear, and filled with a large dose of control and manipulation. It is important to look at your spiritual leaders closely. Some people who become religious or spiritual authorities crave, live off, and relish the power this gives them over other people's lives. Because of the adulation they receive, they can easily begin to feel as though they are larger than life, have been divinely called, know the final answer, and can do whatever they like. If you look closely, so much of the behavior of these religious and spiritual authorities is often contradictory to the beliefs and texts they so adamantly defend. When anyone is harmed, shamed, punished, ostracized, or humiliated in the name of a religious or spiritual practice, it is the result of manipulation and control. This is not true practice, but spiritual abuse.

If you are under the influence of authority figures whose dogmatic beliefs cannot be questioned, you are not in the presence of true spiritual leaders. When you take your authority back from these negative figures, however—when you see them not as religious authorities, but as the hooligans, charlatans, hysterics, or power-hungry individuals they often are—you have made the first step in untying the golden chains that have shackled you. You have taken back the richness and healing power of true spiritual practice and have made it your own.

WHAT is your spiritual practice? How do you deal with the fundamental questions of life? Where do you turn for answers? Does this practice respect you, offer you a chance to explore and grow? Or are you under constriction to blindly obey and fit in?

Untying the Golden Chains

On the road to fearlessness, we must untie the chains that bind us to relentless authority, dogmatic beliefs, and blind obedience. This is not to say that obedience is necessarily negative—not if we have *chosen* who or what we wish to obey. But blind obedience that is thrust upon us, dogmatic beliefs that we do not have the opportunity to explore and *decide* about for ourselves, keep us living in a fog, easily manipulated. We are discounting and distrusting our own true inheritance, a thinking mind and discerning heart. We are rejecting responsibility for our choices and actions, and just following along. A life like this not only painfully strangles us, but inevitably causes pain for others.

We are warned of this in all religious scriptures. The Hebrew Bible tells us clearly:

> "COME TO ME DIRECTLY, NOT TO MAN WHOSE
> BREATH IS IN HIS NOSTRILS."

The Koran reminds us:

> "TAKE NO OTHERS WITH YOU WHEN YOU GO TO
> WORSHIP GOD. WORSHIP GOD ONLY."

The New Testament proclaims:

> "I AM THE WAY, THE TRUTH, AND THE LIFE.
> WHOSOEVER SEES ME, SEES THE FATHER."

Choose Life

A great step in reclaiming your freedom is rehabilitating your ability to *choose*.

The ability to choose is a great gift. Through choice you take responsibility. It has been said that all the difficulties you are presented with in life are given to you only so that you can become able to choose. Your choices determine your character—you are as you choose. The Bible clearly says: "I have given you two choices, blessing and curse. Choose blessing. Choose Life."

WHAT ARE SOME OF THE MAIN CHOICES you have made in your life? What have the consequences of these choices been? Do you wish to choose again? Do you feel you can? Choose again now.

Choose that which is beneficial. Choose to follow your heart. Choose to stand on your own two feet, open your eyes, your ears, your mind. Most of the time we live as the victims of people, routine, or fate. However, every day we are offered many choices. New choices are like new seeds to plant in the soil of our lives. They require nourishment and care and then, sooner or later, our choices grow into flowers, new opportunities, and circumstances, new displays of courage and love.

The following story is told in many different forms in many different cultures. It captures the essence of your responsibility for taking action and making wise choices in life.

> The river was flooding its banks, and the water was rising around Jim's house. It had gotten to the front porch where he was standing. A man in a rowboat came by and called to him, "Hop in and I'll take you to high ground."
>
> Jim replied, "No, my God will save me!"
>
> He then ran up to the second floor. The river continued to rise to the second-story windows. A man in a powerboat came up and called to him, "Hope in and I'll take you to high ground."
>
> Jim called back to him, "No, my God will save me."
>
> Then Jim ran up to the roof. Soon the river had risen to the top of the house. Jim was sitting on the roof ridge, with the waters swirling around his feet. He saw a helicopter fly over, and the people inside yelled through a bullhorn, "Grab the rope and climb in, and we'll take you to high ground."

Jim called back, "No, my God will save me."

The river continued to rise and finally engulfed the entire house, and Jim drowned.

The next thing he knew, he was standing before God. In anger, Jim asked God, "I put my trust in you. Why have you forsaken me?"

God smiled and replied, "I never forsook you. I sent you a rowboat, a powerboat, and a helicopter. Why didn't you get in?"

WHAT CHOICES DID YOU MAKE TODAY? Were you even aware that a choice was called for, or did you react automatically? Did you choose to take action? Did you choose kindness—to go out of your way, communicate honestly, respond from the fullness that you are?

The more you choose, the less you need authority figures to decide and provide *their* answers to *your* life's questions.

You have been given not only the gift of choice, *but the gift of speech and hearing.* These are enormous tools, which you can use to put an end to manipulation and control. Do you use them? Do you truly say what you mean, ask for what you need, and know how to both listen and hear? Are you available for the communications others make to you, or do you live in your own fearful dream world?

Communication

Jill feels safe to be angry with Jack
because Jack does nothing
She is angry with Jack
because he does nothing
She is angry with Jack
because he does not frighten her
He does not frighten her
Because, doing nothing, he is useless.
She feels safe with him.

—*R. D. Laing,* Knots

A great deal of manipulation and control take place through communication that has gone awry. Someone says or does one thing and means another. You become confused about what is going on, and through your confusion you are weakened and manipulated. Promises are made that are not kept. Words are said that have no substance. People who sense your deepest needs dangle you on a string—seduce, tease, and tantalize you, with no ability or intention to deliver what they promised.

But all pretenses are eventually transparent. No matter how much you play-act, your deeper communications are always being heard—and responded to. It cannot be any other way. The real question here is, Are you willing to openly face and share your truth with others? When you do, you step right out of the compulsion and into healthy control.

WHO are you most willing to communicate with? Who are you unwilling to communicate with? Why?

Many people complain that they are not understood. Wives complain that their husbands do not communicate. Employees feel that their employers do not listen. Families, too, have their own intricate ways of communicating. Some dedicate all their efforts to keeping each other from knowing the truth. For some people, life is dedicated not to communicating but to hiding, withholding, and presenting a front. These individuals are focused on using their communication as a means of control. The unwillingness to communicate is a form of communication, too.

The Many Facets of Communication

In order to dissolve fear in your life, you must really understand the power that communication has, and how necessary it truly is to be forthright and clear. There are all kinds of communication—communication that brings health and joy; and communication that increases pain and controls and destroys you in different ways. Around some people, plants grow wildly. Around others, they wither and die. Why? Plants don't need a reason. They do not ask questions. They just bloom or die. Despite all your reasoning, you, too, bloom or wither around different individuals. It is important to start noticing this, to be in touch with your visceral responses, rather than concentrating on what you believe you are *supposed* to feel.

Communication has many facets. You talk and listen in many different ways. First there are the words you speak. Then beneath the words, your body language, the subtle messages and movements you make. How are you standing, sitting, moving, or gesturing? How are you dressed? What is your tone of voice like? Are your verbal and non-verbal communication aligned? Are you saying one thing with words and another with your behavior? There are as many different ways of communicating as there are people, and just as many different ways of listening and being heard.

You are told how you are *supposed* to respond to all kinds of communications, how you are *supposed* to feel. Usually, you are expected to like someone because of his merits and dislike him because of his faults. But truthfully, it doesn't work that way. Deep down, you may love the so-called villains and not really feel so good around the so-called saints. It is the fundamental communication being made that matters; your visceral sense knows what's going on. When you learn to trust your visceral sense, you cannot be blindsided or manipulated anymore.

Mystification

> I don't respect myself
> I can't respect anyone who respects me.
> I can only respect someone who does not respect me.
> I respect Jack
> Because he does not respect me.
> I despise Tom
> Because he does not despise me.
> Only a despicable person
> Can respect someone as despicable as me.
> —*R. D. Laing,* Knots

Mystification is another form of manipulation and control—the conscious or unconscious efforts of one person to confuse, mystify, or deny the feelings and perceptions of another person or even his or her own. The main ingredient in abusive relationships, mystification is a toxic form of communication that obscures well-being and tears people down.

ARE YOU WILLING to enter into an honest, open exchange? Or would you rather speak in innuendos and double meanings? This is a choice you have to make.

When you are being mystified, you have the sense of not having any solid ground to stand on. You are receiving two different types of communication simultaneously. You hear one thing with words and another thing non-verbally, or the person says one thing and does the opposite. You don't know which message to respond to. This kind of communication causes paralysis and deep fear. It is the best way to drive someone crazy.

Each of us has the need to be known, to be heard, and to have our experience honored. If you refuse to listen to or absorb confusing communication and mixed messages, you can't be controlled and manipulated. It's important to decode mixed messages and respond to the basic communication that is being made. To do this, you must learn to listen not only to the words you're hearing, but also to the way the communication makes you feel. Some people say that you know the true intention of the communication by noticing the response it elicits.

DISCOVER whether you are using communication to be in touch with other people, or to hide, confuse, or mystify your intentions. What is the underlying message you are sending?

Person to Person

The true nature of your relationships to others is contained in the way you speak to them. It may not be your words that people are responding to, but your tone, which communicates the way in which you view them. Implicitly, no matter what you are saying, you are always communicating what others mean to you, who they are in your world.

The other person may mean nothing to you, and you may speak to him as if he were an object, someone who exists only for your purposes.

This is a highly impersonal communication, delivered in an automatic way. (Some people say "I love you" in just this way.)

In a situation like this, the person you are speaking to will start to shrivel up inside. He will feel bossed, lectured, or pushed around. In severe cases, he may even start to feel as if his life is being drained away. Some bosses speak this way to their employees, as if the employee were not a person, but an object to be used. Under these circumstances, the employees may start to feel as if they do not matter. And the truth is, in the boss's world they do not.

There is another way in which you can relate to others. In this way, you allow yourself to be fully aware that the other is also a person. She has the complete right to feelings and responses of her own. You make room for her uniqueness. You allow her to be who she is, fully welcoming your differences. This kind of relationship can develop into a dialogue.

There are no gifted and ungifted here, only those who give themselves and those who withhold.

—*Martin Buber*

The first kind of relationship, where a person is viewed as an object, is what Martin Buber has called an I–It relationship, where no real communication is possible. You are simply relating to the other person as an object to fulfill your own desires. In the second kind of relationship, where you grant a person her own personhood, what Buber calls an I–Thou relationship, you are opening yourself up to something larger. This can feel dangerous—because it is unpredictable—and you may feel as if something uncontrollable is about to take place. But what is really possible under these conditions is the chance of a real meeting.

Real Meetings

Remember, there's only one reason to do anything,
A meeting with the Friend is the only real
payment.

—*Rumi*

Sometimes you are courageous and able to say yes to whatever is going on. You open your heart, completely let go, and allow everything to be just as it is. You may even be able to allow your own heart to speak out all by itself. Your heart has a language of its own. The voice of the heart is always eager to be heard, and when it simply bursts forth, a real meeting can take place.

A real meeting takes you home to your center. There is no more need to control; your sense of separation vanishes. You see that all are truly one.

Real meetings can happen spontaneously. They can happen for a moment, or last for a while. They can happen between two people, or between a person and the sky, a rock, a bird, a song. You cannot demand that a real meeting happen. But you can learn how to invite it in.

In a real meeting between two people, the most important ingredients needed are two individuals who are real and who are willing to be fully present. For the time of the meeting, each is willing to let go of the need to control. They also forget about wanting praise in the other person's eyes, and their need to be important or right. There is no longer a need to protect themselves; they may even see that there is nothing to protect. This kind of meeting is tremendously liberating. When it happens, you may begin to laugh out loud or cry.

Most of us have experienced a taste of this kind of meeting at one time or another. It is everyone's natural birthright. In order to fully court this kind of interaction, you need to make yourself ready, to invite it in.

Martin Buber describes this kind of meeting beautifully in his book *Between Man and Man:*

It involves two strangers who meet in the early evening on a deserted platform, waiting for a train. They know nothing of one another. One is reading his newspaper. The train arrives and the two enter the train, sit down together, and do not speak.

Suddenly and unexpectedly, the veils over their hearts lift. The usual defensiveness and shut-up-ness they live in dissolves. Without any words being uttered, full communication streams from one person to the next. During this time, each knows everything about the other and both feel as close to the other as to their very selves. Both hearts have opened and spoken; each feels filled and blessed.

Buber says it is as though a spell is lifted and the reserve that people usually enforce upon themselves is released. This allows a true meeting to take place.

This kind of opening is possible for us all. As you prepare for a real meeting, you move into a deeper level of communication. Some call it communion. It is the experience of being in touch with that which is greater than yourself. During communion, you are simply there, in the presence of another or just of life itself. Nothing need be said or done. You are fully available to whatever is happening, and by yielding to it you enter into oneness and love. At that moment, all of life opens, and you see the magnificence of who you truly are.

> Unexpectedly,
> in the
> Florida heat
> The blue heron danced
> For me.
> Lifted one fragile leg
> From the mud,
> Pointed his toes
> And swirled
> For me.
> We fell in love.
> He looked at me
> Glamorously,
> Glad I could see

Could see, could see
Beneath the veil of feathers
And wings
Who lived there truly,
And that he,
In one daring moment,
Swirled around
Spread his wings,
And dared to
fall in love
With me.

—Eshin

TURNING POINT

As You Let Go, You Make Room for the Good That Is to Come

Emerson says that there is a natural law of magnetism that brings to each what truly belongs to them and which is for their greater good. The more you stop controlling life and accept, honor, and welcome it, the more your life will be filled not only with a deep peace of mind, but with the many gifts the universe has in store for you.

SEVEN

PRINCIPLE 7

Discovering Your Perfect Nature: Becoming a Friend

Give up your proud airs, sirs
They won't do you any good
That's all I have to tell you.
—LAO-TZU

MOST OF THE TIME, WE DECIDE how we're doing by comparing ourselves to others. Unless we are on the A-list, come out on top, are the most beautiful, rich, or brilliant, we feel lacking in some way. Our measure of self-worth becomes how much better we are than others, how far we outdo them. Not only do we then have to constantly check how we're doing, but we're not aware how destructive this is to our relationships. People simply become objects to surpass or conquer. Inevitably, this way of living leads to deep loneliness and a life embedded in fear. This is living in the law of the jungle, where only the best and strongest survive.

In a famous Zen story, a man went to a crowded meat store. When his turn came, he demanded, "Hurry up. Give me the best piece of meat."

The butcher laughed and simply answered, "Every piece is the best piece of meat."

When you always have to be better than others, you are living in "scarcity consciousness," the feeling that there is never enough love, praise, success, or money to go around; you have to quickly grab whatever is good, taking it from others. Yet no matter how much you get, it's never enough. And when someone else receives something, you believe there's that much less for you. If they win, you lose.

In this state of mind, it's easy to block out how enormously abundant the universe is, always replenishing itself and giving more. In fact, there is never a lack of praise, success, relationships, or nourishment of any kind. When one person receives, no one else is poorer for it. There is always enough for all. Those embedded in scarcity consciousness project their sense of fundamental emptiness on the world. They have forgotten their true place in life and especially forgotten their Source.

Human happiness comes from perfect harmony with others.

—*Chuang Tzu*

Remembering Your Source

Clea went to one singles party after another, determined to find a top-notch match. Before she even stepped in the door, she'd look other women up and down to see how she stacked up. No one came close. She was the thinnest, prettiest, and sexiest, by far. She wasn't going to lose out, she thought. Then she'd focus on the handsomest, flashiest guys she could find. Basically, Clea wasn't as interested in who these men were as she was in walking away with the prize.

Naturally, even when Clea attracted a man she wanted, the relationship didn't last very long. She never really cared much about him, only winning the battle of love. Clea never learned that love is not a battle. And when the men who'd originally found her appealing sensed the truth, they ran away from her as fast as they could.

Clea's conflict with others, her driving wish to be better than they were, dominated her life because she did not know her own intrinsic value. She had never learned how to become her own best friend. Winning does not come from beating others out of anything; it comes from knowing who you are, why you are here, and what is required of you in your relationships with others. It comes from remembering your Source.

Each of us has a higher nature that is connected to the Source. This higher nature is filled with goodwill and compassion, knows that the world is plentiful, and that it's impossible to lose anything that is really yours. The more you live in your higher nature, the less you will be subject to fear. And as you break free from fear's power over you, your higher nature takes over and guides your life.

Becoming Friends: Everyone Wins

> *Of all the things in life most precious is a meeting with the Friend.*
>
> —Rumi

There are many things we learn as we grow, but few of us learn how to be a true friend. So many relationships are based on rivalry, filled with malice and fear. So many friendships become torn up in conflict, causing sorrow and loss. Two people, who were once bonded, suddenly become adversaries. What was once thought of as love, quickly turns into hate. Each becomes engrossed in winning the battle between them, no matter how much destruction and agony it creates. Once again, this happens because we crave being better than others, being smarter, being right. Power struggles may be familiar, but they are a poor substitute for love.

WHO ARE YOU in conflict with? Why? What do you do to resolve it? Is it working?

All conflict stems from the idea that there can only be one winner and only one person or point of view that can be right. But true success comes from learning what it means to win together, to become a friend. A great step in breaking the chains of fear is to leave power struggles behind and be able to win together all the time.

STOP for a moment and notice how you treat your best friend. Do you treat yourself that way as well? Do you feel you deserve it?

Healing Conflict

> *Any conflict, whether it takes place within the body and mind or outside it, is always a battle against the Self.*
>
> —*Taisen Deshimaru*

Conflict arises when you are accosted by demands and drives that pull you in opposing directions. You can't decide which way to go, what's right, what's beneficial, or what leads to sorrow. You feel you have to accept one side of the conflict and reject the other. Somehow you cannot accept the fullness of all that you are and make room for many possibilities. Like Clea, in the story on page 138, you may try to resolve your inner struggle by trying to win every prize. By being "better" than others, you imagine your conflict is resolved. It isn't. The battle with others has only been a distraction from the real battle going on within.

INNER CONFLICTS AND CONFLICTS WITH OTHERS ARE
TWO SIDES OF THE SAME COIN.

When you do not know who you are and what you truly need, not only do you live in conflict, but you think that winning over others leads to well-being and success. You think that fighting leads to peace. It never happens; fighting leads to more fighting. Beating others out eventually leads to being beat out. It cannot be any other way.

> *All mankind is one family, one people.*
>
> —*Muhammad*

There are many specific constructive steps you can take to truly resolve conflict, to *do* peace and balance your relationship both with others and with yourself. As this happens, your need to live by the law of the jungle subsides. You tap into your inner resources and begin to remember and live from your Source.

How to Get from I to We: Creating a Win-Win Environment

To care for others makes the whole world come to life.

—Kosho Uchiyama Roshi

Win-win relationships are based on mutual support and success. One person does not have to lose for another to win. Each only wins when the other does. An example of a win-win relationship is a couple in the process of divorce fighting about custody of a child they love. Both want the child to thrive. In order for this to happen, both parents must find a way to work together compatibly, not to rip the child apart. When each grants the other the right to happiness and allows the other to have basic needs met, the child does so much better. Ultimately, all win together.

When you feel cared for and supported, you always do your best. Sometimes, surprisingly enough, you have a difficult time allowing yourself to be supported. You may feel it is a sign of weakness. At other times, you may have difficulty extending support. But all healthy relationships are built on mutual trust and support.

Relationship balancing is the natural flow of energy, support, and inspiration between individuals who interact. When this flow is balanced and mutual—like yin and yang—each operates at its optimal level. Natural synchronicity appears, and unexpected resources become available. When this flow is blocked or otherwise out of balance, an energy drain occurs, causing depression, resentment, and destructive behavior. Blocked flow is the perfect soil for conflict to take root.

All individuals, relationships, and organizations naturally seek harmony and balance. There are many ways of achieving this, and one of them is conflict. Conflict is not always negative; it can be a means of establishing a new balance when old ways of interacting are no longer effective. When change and growth are needed, conflict arises in order to expedite the changes needed.

Actually, it is not difficult to create an environment where everyone can win. There are basic principles to follow and simple steps to take. Although these steps and principles may be different from what you are accustomed to, by giving them a chance, you will discover a whole new world. It takes a conscious effort to undo the law of the jungle. As you consciously create this new lifestyle, however, not only does it become easy to resolve conflict, but fear and stress melt away and incredible results appear in your life.

Win-Win Relationships

A few years ago, at the Seattle Special Olympics, nine contestants, each physically or mentally challenged, assembled at the starting line for the hundred-yard dash. At the gun, they all started out, not exactly in a dash, but with excitement, to run the race to the finish and win.

All, that is, except one boy, who stumbled on the asphalt, tumbled a couple of times, and began to cry. The other eight heard the boy cry. They slowed down and looked back. They all turned around then and went back. Each one of them.

One girl with Down syndrome bent down and kissed him and said, "This will make it better." All nine linked arms and walked across the finish line together. Everyone in the stadium stood, and the cheering went on for several minutes. People who were there are still telling the story. Why? Because deep down we know one thing: What matters in this life is more than winning for ourselves. What truly matters is helping others win, even if it means slowing down and changing our course.

Who Is the Competitor?

We all react differently to competition. You may behave as those described in the story above, and see a competitor as a partner in life's race. Your deepest wish may be for everyone to thrive.

Or you may feel that competition is a stimulus to do your best. For you, competition is healthy, and you enjoy the opportunity to reach new plateaus and try as hard as you can.

You might also have a different response: You might choose to hide, withdraw, and refuse to take the challenge. When a competitor appears on the scene, you may feel like a failure and give up long before the competition begins.

Finally, you may be one who, sensing competitors, tries to wipe them out. You see competitors as dangerous, malevolent, as predators who have come to take your good away. A predator is a competitor who has a personal vendetta against you or wishes to actively undermine and harm you. This person may be jealous, suspicious, unstable, or vengeful. It is crucial to know who is who, because you can react to competitors as if they are predators when they are not. This confusion blocks your ability to harness your energy and be clear about how to respond.

WRITE FIVE POSITIVE things about competition in your life. When did a competitor help you to become more than you thought you could be?

Facing a predator requires different responses from facing healthy competitors. There is a difference between being threatened and being challenged, and you need to know which is which.

When you are genuinely up against a predator, where there is personal anger, abuse, or emotional instability, it is appropriate to take other measures than with a healthy competitor. You never need to panic, however, because many sources of responsible help are available.

LIST THE INDIVIDUALS you consider predators in your life. Make a list of your competitors. How are they different?

Undo Silent Killers

Silent killers are people whose communications and behaviors take your enthusiasm, courage, and strength away. They have also been called energy drains and hidden potholes you can fall into. The fact that they are silent means that they have gone unnoticed or denied. Denial itself is a huge silent killer. Denial is pretending that something is not happening, while all the time you are suffering the effects of it.

TAKE TIME every day to note when and where you feel yourself losing strength, courage, joy, or aliveness—when you feel undermined. Who was present, what did they say you? Awareness takes the power of denial away.

Everyone has different silent killers in their lives. The event may seem silly or insignificant—a minor remark, a moment when you feel overlooked. You may feel embarrassed to acknowledge the huge power these killers have over you. By their very nature silent killers are subtle; if they weren't, you would have been aware of them a long time ago. They are often small events, comments, or omissions that you barely register. What you suddenly *do* notice and feel, though, is loss of energy, depression, or upset. By becoming vigilant and noticing whatever is going on around you, when these reactions occur, you are tracking down your particular silent killers and beginning the work of defusing them.

Dissolve Misunderstandings

In order to build a win-win environment, misunderstandings must be dealt with on the spot. When misunderstandings are allowed to fester, they create havoc. Resentments build, obsessions grow, relationships become tangled. Take charge of communications, respond to what you've heard or think you've heard. Do it on the spot.

Remember, there may be worlds between what you've heard and what the other person actually meant. Feedback is crucial. You may be too proud to ask for feedback or to give it. You immediately assume you know what has been said. Most of the time you are off course.

As soon as any misunderstanding develops, realize that mis-communication may be at the bottom of it. A feedback loop is required. This can instantly short-circuit bad feelings. If you notice that there's been a misunderstanding, say, "I would like to clarify what I think I've heard you say." Then the other person can communicate what it was he or she meant.

Just the willingness to clarify the communication, and not blame the other person, is an overt act of friendship and goodwill and is usually received as such. It gives you the opportunity to make corrections. From here further communication often takes place naturally.

Often a misunderstanding arises due to disappointment. When someone disappoints you, a common response is to withdraw and become unwilling to communicate.

BECOME AWARE of what it is you need to feel respected and secure in a relationship. If this is being constantly undermined, notice it. Honor your needs and communicate them.

Quickly communicating what is true for you in a situation has magical effects. In the beginning it can be difficult, but over time it is a wonderful tool for building relationships that are sure to grow.

Other Ways of Defusing Conflict

It's easy to be too hasty in deciding that someone is a predator or a silent killer. Before you decide this, seek to defuse the situation. Try to find all that is positive in the person. Do not look on him or her with negative eyes. When you do not add fuel to the fire and when you constantly see the positive, others often respond in kind.

———

The way you see people
Is how you treat people
How you treat people
Is what they become.

—*Goethe*

———

You can also defuse negativity by not responding to taunts. The person may then lose interest, and the situation can calm down. Other times this is not possible, and you must take action. It is always best to do this through proper channels, in an impersonal way.

The great samurai Tsukahara Bokuden was a master swordsman who in his career crossed swords with as many as two hundred samurai, defeating them all. He also founded his own school of fencing.

On one occasion Master Bokuden was traveling by boat with a few other passengers. One was a particularly crude and belligerent samurai, who was boasting about his great fencing skills to anyone who would listen. Naturally, Master Bokuden was completely uninterested in such bravado. He went to the other side of the boat and took a little nap.

After a while the braggart noticed Master Bokuden's complete disregard for his antics. The lack of attention angered the samurai. He went over and shook Master Bokuden's shoulder rudely and asked, "How is it that you are so uninterested in fencing that you choose to take a nap?

Master Bokuden responded politely. "My art is quite different from yours. It consists of not defeating others and not being defeated by others."

The samurai grew even more angry. "What's the name of your fencing school," he shouted.

Master Bokuden replied, "Mine is known as the No Hands School. This means we defeat the enemy without resorting to our sword."

"Why then do you carry a sword?" asked the samurai.

"This sword," answered Master Bokuden, "is not for defeating others. It is for doing away with my own selfish motives."

By now the samurai was livid. "So! You expect to fight me without using your sword?"

"Why not?" responded Master Bokuden.

The samurai immediately instructed the boatman to steer toward the nearest island where this matter could be settled at once. Master Bokuden cautioned against this, suggesting a more remote island where there would be less possibility of any bystanders being hurt.

The boatman complied and steered toward a remote island. As the boat entered the shallow water around the island, the samurai, eager for combat, jumped out of the vessel, drew his sword, and waded to the beach.

Back in the boat, Master Bokuden calmly removed his swords. He handed them to the boatman as the samurai disembarked.

Suddenly Master Bokuden grabbed the boatman's oar and pushed it against a rock, sending the boat off into deep water. As the boat glided away from the island and the now stranded samurai, Master Bokuden explained, "This is my No Hands School."

—*Neil Dunnigan*

Vitamins and Minerals for the Heart, Mind, and Soul

Vitamins and minerals for the heart, mind, and soul are thoughts, behaviors, feelings, and choices that will strengthen not only you, but everyone else with whom you come in contact. They include specific actions, and together build a foundation for a life that is constructive and nurturing. Living on this basis, you can never be shaken, no matter what storm comes along. You are in alignment with your Source.

What follows is a series of vitamins and minerals for your heart, mind, and soul. Take them as suggested, and see how strong you become.

> A traveler came to a banquet where there were two large rooms. In one room starving people sat at the table, eating all they could. They seemed agitated. The traveler asked why they were upset, and someone there told him that the people at the table were all in hell.
>
> He then went to the next room, in which everyone sat at the table happily and at ease. The traveler asked why they were so happy. Someone said, "In the other room, where the people are in hell, they are busy feeding themselves. Here we feed one another, and are in heaven."
>
> —*Zen story*

• THE POWER OF ACKNOWLEDGMENT

No matter how hard he tried, Paul never felt appreciated. Even when he made big sales at work, nothing much was said. He began to find it difficult to go on, and wondered why he was losing enthusiasm. When a new team leader was appointed to his group and began to regularly acknowledge not only Paul's success, but his daily efforts, Paul became unstoppable. He didn't feel invisible anymore; he felt that what he did mattered.

Acknowledging others is like giving water to a thirsty plant. When you acknowledge someone, you offer honest, positive feedback about what they've done that has been meaningful or uplifting to you.

Everyone thrives when they are acknowledged, yet most of the feedback we receive has to do with what we have done wrong. Acknowledgment is a simple, but extremely powerful force that allows you to feel appreciated, respected, and supported, rather than torn down.

You can acknowledge someone easily by simply saying, *"Something I want to acknowledge you for is . . ."*—and say it. Then let it sink in. Don't wait for any particular response. Let your acknowledgment be freely given and freely received. Acknowledge others for as many things as you can, on an ongoing basis. And take the time to stop and acknowledge yourself as well. Notice and appreciate your positive actions and your accomplishments. Take a moment to thank yourself also. You will feel nourished and uplifted and inspired to do more.

• NEVER GIVE UP ON A PERSON
(LOJONG PRACTICE, TIBETAN BUDDHISM)

It's so easy to give up on others when they begin to make mistakes or offend you in some way. You may do this before you know who they really are and what they're ultimately capable of doing. However, if you can stick with them through thick and thin, the people you are in relationship with will feel safe to grow and learn. They will realize that mistakes are not fatal, but a natural part of the process of learning.

When a person is free to make mistakes and not be punished for it, the level of commitment and creativity in the relationship grows beyond all expectation. By giving someone this degree of support, you allow the person's potential to be realized, and you learn patience and endurance as well. You also learn not to be hasty in judging others; each of us has enormous gifts that will flower under the right conditions.

In Zen practice, periods of intense training are called sesshins. They can last from one to seven days or more, with Zazen (meditation) going on from four or five in the morning to late at night. Silence is kept. No one is allowed to come or go during this period. The intensity builds as each day goes by and practice deepens.

Similar to mountain climbing, as the days pass and you get closer to the peak, all kinds of obstacles arise. No matter what happens, however, you are expected to sit still, go through the difficulty, and come out the other side. My beloved teacher, a Japanese samurai Zen master, is a wonderful example of this kind of courage. For years I watched him persist and endure everything that came into his life, no matter how difficult.

However, during many years of attending these sesshins, I did what many there would consider unimaginable—I ran away many times. Before I decided to go, the pain or difficulty seemed to be unbearable. All I could think of was leaving, getting as far away as I could. At first when I ran away I felt huge relief, thrilled to be out of there, vowing never to return again. I would drive to the closest diner, sit drinking coffee, and congratulate myself on having been smart enough to leave.

After a while, driving home, a sense of bleakness pervaded my heart. Another opportunity lost. I realized there was nowhere to run—I took these issues with me wherever I went. Inevitably, time after time, I returned to the Zen Center to resume practice, as usual.

My Zen master never once said one word to me about it, not for more than thirty years. Even when I gave up on myself, he never gave up on me. I would return and, as if nothing happened, we would simply pick it up from there.

What made it possible for him to respond in that manner? What huge strength and dedication had he discovered to honor life so profoundly?

• **GIVE OTHERS THE BENEFIT OF THE DOUBT**
Do not look at the faults of others,
Look at your own deeds,
Done and undone.

—*Buddha*

When someone offends you, before you start to judge and create all kinds of terrible stories, give the person the benefit of the doubt. Don't take what was said personally; find alternative, positive explanations for why things happened as they did. These explanations may seem like a stretch at first, but they are powerful medicine in keeping you calm, allowing you to see other aspects of the situation, and offering kindness and mercy.

• LET OTHERS BE RIGHT

Let everyone be right. Tell yourself, *I have plenty of time to be right tomorrow; today it is their turn.* When you are willing to concede that others can be right, even if they differ from you, you are making space in your life for openness, variety, and the willingness to grow. What other people do can be right *for them.* You can be right as well. There need not be pain and conflict over this—there's room for everyone to live a life that feels correct for them.

• STOP CASTING BLAME

It is easy and natural to blame others for your own difficulties, failures, or lack of self-esteem. When you do, however, you are the one being disempowered. By blaming others, you prevent yourself from seeing your part in the situation, what you are doing to keep things going, and what you could do to create a change.

• LET GO OF RESENTMENT

When you refuse to let go of the wrongs you feel have been done to you, resentment builds and fuels conflict. Not only does this shut you down, but anger expressed toward others always returns, one way or another, to you.

• GIVE UP UNREALISTIC HOPES AND EXPECTATIONS

Most expectations are simply wishes or dreams. When these expectations conflict with what is actually happening, it can cause upset, fury, sorrow, and pain. It can leave you feeling like you've been betrayed. You can shut down, refuse to play, or take it out on everyone else.

STOP FOR A MOMENT and notice that life happens the way it does. Are you willing to greet it just as it is? Could you let some of your expectations subside and be available to see what's truly going on? When you can, conflict fades away.

- **BECOME CLEAR ABOUT APPROPRIATE AND INAPPROPRIATE DEMANDS**

It may be difficult to sort out appropriate and inappropriate demands. You may fight, resist, and procrastinate because you feel the demands being made of you are not fair. Or you may be secretly resentful at not having your own needs met. Perhaps it's hard for you to say no to others because you feel you are rejecting them. *No* is not a rejection of another, but setting a boundary that can be appropriate and beneficial for both of you. For example, little children want to eat candy all day long. Saying no to them is not harmful. Don't be afraid of saying no.

- **ASK FOR YOUR NEEDS TO BE MET**

Conflict often arises as a way to get your needs met. In the past, you may have asked for what you needed covertly, by manipulating, sulking, demanding, or withholding. You may have refused to ask for what you wanted. You expected others to magically know what your needs were and became upset when they didn't. Of course, this is how a child feels with his parents. He wants them to know his every need and fulfill it immediately. It can be difficult to realize, as you grow, that it is necessary to let your partners know what is needed. It is not proof that they do not love you if you have to ask. It is impossible to deal with conflict wisely if you are unable to ask for what you need and want.

- **ALLOW YOURSELF TO SUCCEED**

Many can't allow themselves to succeed because being successful or powerful may seem dangerous. Some feel safer making themselves helpless and weak. These individuals often sabotage both their own efforts and yours. The easiest way to sabotage a situation, of course, is to constantly create conflict. Fear takes over then, and rather than flourishing as you were intended to, you diminish yourself and cut yourself short.

• TURN A COMPETITOR INTO A FRIEND

Find someone you're competing with and arrange to take her to lunch. Make the lunch all about the other person. Let her be the star and tell you all about her, her life, her hopes, dreams, and fears. Let her shine. Think of ways in which you can help her. By the end of the lunch, this person will no longer seem threatening. Instead, you will spontaneously see ways in which the two of you can support each other, how some of your needs are mutual, and the ways in which you can work together for the benefit of both. Then the need to eliminate this person, or come out on top of her, will dissolve naturally.

• REMEMBER THAT EACH OF US IS BORN WITH OUR OWN PARTICULAR GIFTS AND STRENGTHS

Feeling good about yourself because you are "better than others" is ultimately baseless. Not only that, it keeps you from friendship, love, and true support. The compulsion to compare comes from unwillingness to see the strength and beauty in all of life. All day today, let everyone you see be beautiful and let them be perfect, just as they are.

The roses under my window make no reference to former roses or to better ones. They are what they are. They exist with God today.

—*Ralph Waldo Emerson*

TURNING POINT

The Best Way to Get Rid of Enemies Is to Make Them into Friends

When you hate your enemies and love your friends, when you decide a person is for or against you, you are placing that person in a fixed, static role in your mind. You are not taking into account the fact that change is constant, and that growth and transformation are at the root of life. Those who were once your enemies can change and, one day, become your friends. It is important to see all aspects of them and allow them to grow and change. Living this way, you are not dominated by fear and judgments and soon will be living in a world of friends.

PART 2

BECOMING WHOLE

EIGHT

Finding the Precious Jewel

The precious jewel we have lost,
Some say it is to the East of us,
Some to the West.

—*Kabir*

WHAT IS THE PRECIOUS JEWEL WE HAVE LOST? Where is it hiding? All of us feel we have lost something precious and intrinsic to our lives, but have no idea what it is. The search for this treasure goes on endlessly, in all kinds of ways. Some run to the East looking for it, others to the West. We search all corners of the earth for wealth, relationships, success, approval. Sometimes we even think we've found "it," but usually the pleasure is temporary and we are back searching once again. The search itself can create disappointment and fear. We fear we are missing something important, not living our lives fully.

However, the more we seek the precious jewel outside ourselves, the farther it recedes. It's even possible to begin to believe the precious jewel doesn't exist, that all searching is pointless and leads nowhere. It is crucial to know where to look, and what it is we are so deeply seeking.

When you stop searching you certainly save yourself a lot of mental energy.

—*Zen saying*

In Greek mythology, Sisyphus was assigned the task of rolling a huge boulder up a steep hill. When he got it to the top, it rolled back down. He then had to roll it back up again. This went on endlessly. Like Sisyphus, we carry our hunger with us, struggling to reach the top of the mountain to find satisfaction. At times we even get there. Then, like Sisyphus, sooner or later we see everything roll back down again. Sooner or later, circumstances alter, things unravel, and we're back where we started. Then we start all over again.

Most of us would say that the precious jewel we are seeking, trudging up and down the mountain, is the experience of oneness and love. But why is the search so difficult? Perhaps because we do not know what we're looking for, don't know the difference between real and counterfeit love. This section describes the difference between real and counterfeit love and sets the course for a journey toward healing the separation and finding oneness in life.

———

Love is wanting for the other what they want for themselves,
Even though you may not be the one able to give it to them.

—Virginia Lloyd

———

The Difference Between Real and Counterfeit Love

Counterfeit love is the idea that love is a feeling, not a way of life. It confuses the experience of excitement, infatuation, dependence, and attachment with love. As soon as you have strong feelings toward someone, you feel, delightedly, that you are in love. At long last your longings and dreams will be fulfilled.

This is the feeling of the child—who believes she has finally found the ideal parent who will fulfill all her desires. Now she'll never have to be alone again.

However, when you use another person as an object to fulfill your own desires, it is not love.

When your partner says, "I love you so much I can't live without you," this is not necessarily love. It may be a sign of how insecure or possessive he is, or how afraid he is of being abandoned and lonely. But another person can never give you more than you give yourself. No one can make up for the love you didn't have as a child. Another person can, however, become a source of addiction, a way to stop feeling the sorrow within.

> *Frank fell in love regularly. That part wasn't hard. At first, the new girlfriend seemed to be exactly what he was looking for— she was beautiful, smart, and fun. In the beginning, whatever Frank said went. He made all the plans. She never gave him a hard time.*

> *But after a few months, things would start to change subtly. She would be late for dates, didn't seem quite as happy, and wanted to make some plans as well. Before long, she didn't look quite so pretty. Where was that beautiful girl he met a few months ago who treated him like a prince? He wondered where the love went.*

As soon as the infatuation period subsides—usually six months or so—and reality surfaces, there comes the common refrain: "I don't know where the love went." Of course the love didn't go anywhere. Only the illusion disappeared, as all illusions must. When this happens, Frank, like Sisyphus, simply returns to the mountain and starts climbing again, looking for someone else.

"She's out there somewhere," Frank would say. "I know that sooner or later I'll find that person who will make my life complete."

Frank expects another person to fill the emptiness inside. The simple truth is that no one else can take his emptiness away. Once the person leaves, or the relationship alters, the emptiness reappears. You are the one who must find where your precious jewel is hiding. And there is no need to wait for that special person either. You can open your heart right now. When you do, you will discover that every person is the right person to love. There is never a need to feel lonely.

We are so accustomed to seeking our precious jewel in others that most of us have no idea how to stop and look within. However, there are a few simple laws of love that can serve as guideposts on your journey. These laws of love will keep you from living the life of Sisyphus, repeating the same steps over and over again, and getting caught in the same mirages and snares. These laws of love guard your precious energy and allow your search for the precious jewel to bear rich fruit.

Richard Schiffman, a seeker, author, and poet, went to India to find a teacher who would lead him to his precious jewel—direct experience of God and love. He spent some years in different centers and then was led to a place that would become his true home—the House of All, in Jillellamudi, South India. In an interview about his book *The Mother of All*, he describes how he found the precious jewel in his life:

> In Jillellamudi Village, South India, there lived a mother. She fed her children, nursed them in illness, chided them, cajoled them, and comforted their distress. Quite ordinary in appearance, she seemed very much like others, no quirks of character to set her apart. If it were not for one distinctive trait, she would have hardly been noticed, much less worshipped, as she was by untold thousands who eventually came to visit her.
>
> What was it that distinguished this mother from all others? Simply this: Where usually, we limit our deepest love and affection for our biological family, the Mother at Jillellamudi felt that all were her children—all men, women, animals. She cherished and treated everyone equally, with tender care. I never saw Mother reject or discard anyone. Whoever came to her, she saw only her child appearing, with myriad names, conditions, and forms.
>
> From a young age, Mother came to this world with unusual wisdom and love. When asked who she was, she said, "I am the mother of all."
>
> Miraculous phenomena manifested frequently around her during her early years.
>
> Later on, when asked again who she was, she said with a smile, "I am the mother who cannot be wounded."
>
> Nothing anyone did could hurt or upset her.

During the four years I had the blessing to live with Mother, I saw that she could not be shaken from her firm base of love and kindness to all. There was an absolute calm in her countenance and a radiance about her. When you came into her presence for the first time she looked at you with a look of surprising familiarity, as if she knew you already; you were not a stranger at all.

You had only to sit with her for a short time to see why so many were drawn to her. Every day an unending stream passed through her small rooms. It seemed that the full burden of the world's joys and sorrows got poured out daily at Mother's feet. And always she listened patiently, with a rare concern that never seemed to wane. For each and every one she had affectionate words, a smile or maternal caress, and the gift of her total attention.

It is remarkable that, despite the large number of visitors, everyone left with the impression that Mother had a special place in her heart for him or her alone. The truth is that each one was irredeemably precious to her, a beloved child. It was soon apparent that Mother's love was not the marketplace sort, flattering, bribing, seeking to possess, or demanding a fair return on investment. On the contrary, there wasn't the least compulsion or attachment. It just was—like the earth is, the air, open, fluid. And like the air, her love was profoundly free and left the recipient free as well.

All kinds of people came to visit. Some challenging and disturbed. However, Mother reacted to everyone in exactly the same way. I once saw a man who wanted to test Mother lunge at her with a knife. She did not flinch in the slightest, but kept looking at him with love. He broke down and sobbed, asking to become her devotee. Mother accepted him with a full heart.

"Whether they throw rocks or throw flowers, it's all the same to me," Mother said. Whatever was given to her, Mother accepted as a gift.

Mother usually sat quietly on her cot, rarely stepping out of her austere apartment, almost never leaving Jillellamudi. She did not give speeches or write books. She spent hours at a time on her cot in silence or light talk as people filed by, offering respect or receiving her blessing. Yet steadily, through the silent influence of her total love, the lives of many were transformed.

The more you draw close to the kind of love Mother expressed, the more you see that beneath the seeming madness of the world, all is in harmony and all is well. Your work is to realize and rest in that. Once you do, your search has ended; the precious jewel is in your hands.

The Simple Laws of Love

Through love all that is bitter will be sweet
Through love, all that is copper will be gold
Through love all dregs will turn to purest wine
Through love all pain
Will turn to medicine.
Through love the dead will all become alive.

—*Rumi*

The process of becoming fearless is a process of learning how to live a life based in love. This is a life of practice, based upon actions that will open your heart, clear your mind, and make you available to all that is waiting for you.

The simple laws of love are antidotes to fear of every kind. As you learn and practice these laws, your peace of mind will grow, and your fears will dissolve on the spot. Then you'll see for yourself how powerful and healing even a little drop of love can be.

Before you walk on these stepping-stones, it is useful to realize that despite your wish for love, the childish mind within wants to continually ride the roller coaster of life, enjoy itself at the house of horrors. It wants to be thrilled, scared, jumping all night long. To find a taste of true love, the childish mind must evolve and replace its craving for thrills with a desire to know real fulfillment.

When love arrives, it is calm, deep, soothing, nourishing. It does not falter and cannot be taken away. Love stills the roughest waters and brings the best out in everyone. It is the most direct healing for discord of all kinds. When true love arrives, fear vanishes on the spot.

The laws of love are simple. If you follow them they will take you home, where you belong. All you need is a little guidance in practicing them.

• STOP SEEKING OUTSIDE YOURSELF

The musk is inside the deer,
But the deer does not look for it,
It wanders around looking for grass.

—Kabir

It is difficult to go against your usual patterns and change the momentum of your life. In the beginning, you might feel as if you are swimming upstream. When you're accustomed to looking for your needs to be met by someone or something outside of yourself, it may be hard to stop and just sit down. However, when the momentum of your life has not brought what you want, it is time to turn around and look in another direction. It is time to stop racing around and look within.

Franz Kafka, a great author, said that all of our troubles come from not being able to be in a room alone with ourselves. The very first relationship you must establish is with yourself.

Most are not used to being alone with ourselves, and it can seem frightening. Hidden feelings and thoughts can arise, along with the dreaded experience of loneliness. However, there is a huge difference between loneliness and aloneness.

WHEN YOU ARE ABLE TO BE TRULY ALONE WITH YOURSELF, LONELINESS VANISHES. LONELINESS ONLY ARISES BECAUSE YOU CANNOT BE ALONE.

RELISH YOUR ALONENESS. Learn what aloneness truly is and how to cultivate it. Who are you when you are alone? What is your heart saying? Beneath your aloneness something new and powerful is waiting to be revealed.

> I said to the wanting creature inside me,
> What is the river you want to cross?
>
> —*Kabir*

Our entire lives are driven by effort; first we do one thing and then the next. This often escalates into struggle, fighting desperately for what we want. Some of us spend our entire lives struggling harder and harder to achieve a goal. It appears that personal effort and will are the answer. It may seem inconceivable to put all this to a stop, to sit down and do nothing for a while.

In Neal Dunnigan's *Zen Stories of the Samurai,* we learn how crucial it is to develop patience and be able to wait until the perfect moment comes.

A well-known sword master was not pleased with his son Matajuro's progress in fencing. He attributed it to his son's lack of effort. This angered and embarrassed the father, who sent his son to see the famous sword master Banzo.

When Matajuro arrived at the hut of Master Banzo, he was interviewed by the master, who said, "I agree with your father, you do not have the makings of a top swordsman. You will probably never achieve mastery of the art."

"But what if I train arduously? Then how long will it take me to become a master swordsman?" Matajuro pleaded.

"The rest of your life," replied Master Banzo.

"I can't wait that long," protested Matajuro. "I will accept any hardship, devote myself totally."

"Oh, in that case," replied Master Banzo, "it will take ten years."

"What if I train twice as hard?" tried Matajuro.

"Then it will take thirty years," replied Master Banzo.

"What? First you say ten, then you say thirty years. I do not have that much time. I must accomplish this within my father's lifetime."

"With that attitude, I expect it will be closer to seventy years," concluded Master Banzo.

Doing nothing is not passive. You choose to do nothing, to rest in the state of mind where there is nowhere to go, no one to see, no game to win, no demands at all. You are willing to let go, to be who you are, and to allow the greater wisdom and love to lead the way.

———

Sitting quietly,
Doing nothing
Spring comes
And the grass grows
By itself.

—*Ancient Zen poem*

———

Your efforts will not make the grass grow, and yet it grows lavishly. By doing nothing, you relinquish your claim that *you* are the one who runs the world. By doing nothing, you also replenish your own energy and spirit, and allow what is yours to come to you. This is vital, active, constructive. As you quiet the restless, seeking mind, a new life appears. When you stop creating ripples in the water, you can see where the precious jewel lies.

BE QUIET AND STILL. Step out of the chaos for a few moments, or hours, or days. Get off the merry-go-round and roller coaster of your life. Sit at home on a cushion or chair, or sit on a park bench. Just be still. Expect nothing, wait for nothing, be no one, just be, just breathe. Pay attention to your every breath. Without the next one you would not even be here. Whoever said that just being was not enough, that it was not everything?

You know how to find the precious jewel of your life. You know who you are and what is needed. You have always known and always will know. No one else can teach you. No one else can hurt you. You are the prize you are seeking, just as you are.

Doing nothing is a form of meditation, where you put an end to conditioned behavior and reactions and begin the great work of acceptance of all aspects of yourself. At first it can be shocking to look within, face your thoughts, feelings, fantasies. But as you do this daily, you become stronger, wiser, and eventually at home in the amazing world within. During this process you make friends with the rejected aspects of yourself, see what gifts they wish to bring to you. These rejected aspects of yourself cause you to struggle blindly, like Sisyphus. As you do nothing but accept everything within, you heal the division, struggle, and loneliness you have been living with for years.

- **LIVE MINDFULLY**

Wake up and be my friend, sleeping butterfly.

—Zen poem

Mindfulness is another word for being awake to where you are and what is needed of you. As you live mindfully, you allow your attention to be in the moment, just where you are, each step of the way. You take care of everything in your world: flowers, shoes, animals, people. Wide awake, you see to it that everything goes where it belongs. Most of us keep ourselves tremendously busy in order to avoid doing this. When a great Zen Master was asked what Zen was, he said, "Picking up your coat and putting it where it belongs."

BE MINDFUL. Be aware of where you are, what you're doing, and what is needed in the moment. Feel how the air feels on your face, the ground under your feet. When you are cooking, pay attention completely to cooking; whatever you do, pay attention completely. Wake up. Don't lose your life in dreams.

In the beginning, this can seem annoying. Soon it will become second nature. But giving yourself, the world, and others your full unbridled attention is really a form of giving love.

Mindful attention is at the heart of life and of Zen practice. In the following story, we see how this lifelong practice pervades everything.

After ten years of apprenticeship, Tenno achieved the rank of Zen teacher. One rainy day, he went to visit the famous Zen Master Nan-in. When he walked in, the master greeted him with a question: "Did you leave your wooden clogs and umbrella on the porch?"

"Yes, said Tenno.

"Tell me," the Master continued, "did you place your umbrella to the left of your shoes, or to the right?"

Tenno did not know the answer. He realized that he had not yet attained full awareness. So, on the spot, he became Nan-in's apprentice and studied under him for ten more years.

The more mindful you become, the less fantasies take over and the more you see who you are. It can be painful to see who you truly are. It is easy to feel you must become someone else, perfect in some way. This intense craving for perfection, for being someone other than who you are, not only robs you of happiness but hides your precious jewel as well.

Where's the Perfect Person Hiding?

The search to be or find the perfect person can take all your joy in life away. It becomes impossible to rest unless this goal is achieved. No matter how good everything is, something always seems to be missing. This is a cruel joke you play on yourself. If you actually sit down and take a look at who this perfect person is that you're seeking, things turn around.

TAKE A MOMENT to see clearly who a perfect person is to you. Write down all the qualities such a person would have.

By looking at this closely, you might discover that you don't really *like* this perfect person at all. He or she may only be an ego ideal—someone to build up your own self-image. If you do not fit this image or find anyone who does, you might even feel as if your life was not worthwhile.

Buddha Nature Pervades the Entire Universe

In Zen we say, "Buddha nature pervades the entire universe, existing right here, right now."

What is Buddha nature? This is a koan, a question that does not have a logical answer, but must be understood and experienced directly. As you look within, you will taste Buddha nature directly for yourself. This taste is wholly, thoroughly delicious and fulfilling. Once tasted, it is impossible to hunger for anything else. All contrived images of perfection fly away.

Buddha nature is never separate from the moment or from who you are. It has nothing to do with any ideas of how you or someone else "should be." When you taste Buddha nature, it is easy to realize that you are always good enough, always complete; there is nothing to be added or taken away.

Once you begin to accept yourself as you are, even with so-called negative qualities, a magical thing happens: Compassion develops effortlessly along with the ability to give.

REAL LOVE NEVER QUALIFIES, NEVER REJECTS,
DEMANDS. IT REPLENISHES. IT IS LIFE ILLUMINED.

• GIVE COMPLETELY

*Why do we not give ourselves recklessly,
abundantly, completely? We are simply part of an
endless process, have nothing to gain or lose, but
only to live it out.*

—Henry Miller

True giving is love in action. It is not barter, nor does it demand anything in return. When you give in this manner, you don't worry about what is due or what you're getting out of the transaction. That's a business deal, not true giving. True giving is its own reward. This wonderful law of love removes guilt, debt, and obligation and heals anxiety and fear.

The balance between giving and receiving is crucial. When giving is a one-sided interaction, there is a block to healthy flow.

When you find you cannot take from another, something destructive may be going on.

Part of counterfeit love is giving for the purpose of manipulation and control. Some people give in order to hold on to others or feel good about themselves. Others give gifts that are too costly for them and do not know how to receive in return.

When you're lonely, unhappy, or dissatisfied, see what you have not been giving. There's a beautiful saying: "Open your heart if you want love to come into it; open your mind if you want to understand." True giving will change your life completely. Try it today. Give wholeheartedly, wherever needed, to whoever asks. Don't worry about what you're receiving. What's the reason for holding back?

This ancient Zen story epitomizes the ability to give completely, even when we seem to have nothing.

A Zen monk lived alone in a little hut with few possessions. He spent his time meditating and working in his vegetable garden. At night, as he meditated, he felt the beautiful moon shine through his window.

One night two robbers broke in, ransacked his hut, and took all his possessions, including his few, scanty clothes. The Zen monk was left naked, sitting alone on the floor. Then he looked up and noticed the full moon shining in.

"Too bad I can't also give them this beautiful moon," he thought.

As you learn to engage in this kind of giving and receiving, you begin to taste the fruit of real love.

• DEVELOP A GRATEFUL MIND

Naikan, a simple and very powerful practice that developed in Japan, leads to developing a grateful mind.

The basis of this practice is to take careful note of what you receive each day, what you give, and the pain and trouble you cause. Most of the time, you think about how deprived you are, what you do not have. Along with that, it's easy to dwell on how much you give, and to feel burdened or drained. Beyond that, often you dwell on how others have wronged you.

When you do *Naikan*, you turn that all around.

ASK YOURSELF three questions and, carefully and specifically, write your answers down. The first question is, "What have you received today?" The second question, "What have you given today"? The third question, "What trouble or pain have you caused today?"

Once you begin the daily practice of *Naikan*, an interesting thing happens—the scales turn upside down. It often comes as a shock to realize how much you receive and how little you have noticed or acknowledged these gifts. For example, are you aware of receiving the sun in the morning, a delicious breakfast, a smile from a co-worker or friend? Gratitude naturally bubbles up. This is a wonderful cure for depression, since gratitude and depression cannot exist in the same mind at the same time.

Secondly, it can come as a real surprise when you look carefully at what you are actually giving. You suddenly become aware of times you haven't given, when you easily could have. As you do this exercise daily, you naturally want to balance your life and express gratitude for all you receive.

The third question is particularly interesting: What trouble or pain have you caused that day? This question is not intended to create guilt, but awareness. The mind usually concentrates on how it's been wronged. This questions alters that focus and helps you see how you may have caused difficulty to others. When you see this, it is an easy step to make a correction on the spot.

DO THIS EXERCISE ALSO: What have you received from a person, and what have you given? What trouble or pain have you caused? This can be quite startling and can shift things on the spot.

There are *Naikan* retreats where individuals go for a week and do *Naikan* for eight hours a day or more on all aspects of their lives: their relationships, careers, health, dreams.

This exercise trains you to recognize all the good you receive, feel grateful for it, offer thanks, and enjoy giving in return. When you recognize the ways you have caused pain and trouble, rather than feeling guilty, you can correct your errors quickly and be aware so you don't make them again. This is a form of forgiving yourself and developing increased mindfulness as well.

Forgiveness Is the Best Medicine

> *To be wronged or robbed is nothing, unless you continue to remember it.*
>
> —*Confucius*

Some people live their entire lives furious with God, fate, or themselves. They cannot forgive the loss of a loved one, or some great disappointment they had to undergo. We all have a powerful wish for things to turn out as we desire. When this does not happen, anger arises, along with grudges and lack of forgiveness.

But who is so wise to know how things really "should have" happened? Every event has many ramifications and unknown consequences. Out of a painful situation, much good can appear.

A story from the Hasidic Jewish teachings describes how we never truly understand the chain of events in life and how good it is to be grateful for whatever comes.

A rabbi took a trip to a strange land and took a donkey, a rooster, and a lamp with him. As he was refused hospitality in the village inns, he decided to sleep in the woods.

He lit his lamp to study the holy books before going to sleep, but a fierce wind came up, knocking over the lamp and breaking it. The rabbi decided to turn in for the night, saying, "All that God does is for the good."

During the night some wild animals came along and drove away the rooster, and thieves stole the donkey. The rabbi woke up, saw the loss, but still proclaimed easily, "All that God does is for the good."

The rabbi then went back to the village where he had been refused lodging, only to learn that enemy soldiers had invaded it during the night and killed all the inhabitants. He also learned that these soldiers had traveled through the same part of the woods where he lay asleep. Had his lamp not been broken, he would have been discovered. Had not the rooster been chased, it would have crowed, giving him away. Had not the donkey been stolen, it would have brayed. So once more the rabbi declared, "All that God does is for the good."

When you see the good in all situations, there is nothing to forgive. A wonderful way of seeing the good in every situation, whether you like what happened or not, is to *leave the situation as it is*. Don't try to fix or change anything about it. Appreciate it as it is. Watch the situation as if you were watching a film. Give time for the good in it to be revealed.

Letting go in this manner is a form of forgiveness. Forgiveness means to give up. There is no disturbance that forgiveness cannot cure. When you truly forgive another, you give the greatest gift to yourself. You put yourself back into balance and release resentment that poisons every aspect of your life.

You may fear that once you have forgiven, you will be stuck with a person or situation forever. But as you forgive, you do not have to remain in a toxic relationship; you become able to take appropriate action. You can leave the situation with a calm heart. It can be hard to move on when you're in the grip of resentment or fear. Anger creates a strong bond; forgiveness lets go.

Forgiveness is another face of love. It is a practice and needs to be engaged in continually. The simple act of *choosing* forgiveness starts the process going and undoes the pain you are living in. Most importantly, just as with all the deeds of love described, it allows your life to burst into bloom.

> The plum tree
> of my hut,
> It couldn't be helped,
> It bloomed.

> —*Zen poem*

PART 3

WORKSHOP ON
DISSOLVING FEAR

How to Use the Workshop

THIS WORKSHOP IS DEDICATED TO DISSOLVING fear and cultivating love and peace of mind. It is of the utmost importance to do these exercises and work with them in both your life and your community. Given the state of the world today, there is nothing more important to do. The exercises in this workshop (and throughout this book) are simple and enjoyable and more powerful than any weapon you can find. Not only will they keep you safe, but they will be beneficial for those you interact with, as well.

Do the exercises that follow a little bit at a time. The exercises correspond to each chapter in the book. Find those that speak to you. If there's a particular exercise you like, make it your own and do it daily. If need be, go back and read the text for a specific chapter when you work on the exercises.

This workshop will take you on a journey. It takes time and patience. You may find it helpful to work with a partner. Feedback and support are always useful. But even without them, you can still proceed beautifully. Don't make a hard task out of it, but approach it playfully, with curiosity. Some of the exercises or chapters may not resonate with you. That's fine; others will. Don't judge yourself on the results, just keep doing the exercises and reading the material and see what happens in your life.

You have spent your entire life living one way. Don't expect everything to change overnight, but do know that it will change. Persistence and momentum mean a lot. Just keeping "doing it"—day by day, week by week. The simple tasks will transform your life. Beyond everything else, know that you have all you need, right at this moment, to live a fulfilling life. You were not made to cringe in fear or be enslaved by darkness, but to claim the full beauty and power of who you are. I wish you happy journeying.

Meeting Fear Face-to-Face

Refuse False Gifts

Fear doesn't have your best interest in mind, though it pretends to. All of its ways of hooking you in will ultimately take you down.

Take a good look right now at how fear is hooking you in. What false gift is it holding? What is fear promising that it can't deliver—ever? What price are you paying for it?

Let Fear Flow By

Think of a time when a wave of fear washed over you and you did not jump into it but let it flow right by—a time when you saw the truth of the situation, and got in touch with your strength instead. Dwell on this.

Let Fear Change Shape

When you feel your fear, ask what it looks like. Sometimes the feeling morphs into an image. If so, notice the image, see what it means to you. Let the image unfold itself. Thank the image for appearing. Then just watch it. Usually the image changes on its own. As it does, the feeling of fear also alters, and you can see it for what it is—dust in the wind, a passing breeze, powerless, meaningless, and transient.

Keep a Book of Wins

Become aware of every time you've succeeded, despite your fear. Write it down. Every time something positive, valuable, or nourishing happens, even though you were afraid, make note of it. (You can keep a little notebook with you, record these daily, and read them often.) Writing it down helps you stop when something good happens and allows you to taste it fully. Dwell on all the positive events in your life rather than the negative ones.

It's tempting to gloss over the wonderful moments or times when you have succeeded and to focus instead on what's wrong, negative, or still to be done. Now you are giving time, space, and attention to all that is right. Taste it deeply and give thanks. Remember, what you give attention to increases. The more you pay attention to what is positive and nourishing, the more it will increase in your life.

PRINCIPLE 1

The Courage to Be Who You Are

Here are some steps toward self-recovery. They are very simple and yet quite powerful. Do them daily, a little bit at a time. Wait until you've really done one of them before you take on another. Write down what happens as you go along. As you become aware of the wonderful changes that happen, it will encourage you to go on.

1. Take off one mask a day.
What are some of the masks you wear every day? How do you want others to see you? What are you most afraid people will see? What does this fear cost you? Take off one mask a day. Just be as you are for a little while each day. Whatever it is you fear about yourself, spend time daily loving that aspect of yourself. When you fight with and hate a difficult part of yourself, it only makes that part stronger and makes the situation more painful. Welcome the unwanted part of yourself into your life. Look at it with kindness. Give it room to breathe. Let it express itself gently. Allow the truth to be seen and told.

2. Give time and space to what makes you feel happy.
What makes you feel most happy, most deeply fulfilled? (Answer this quickly—just write down whatever comes.) It doesn't matter what others think of it. How much space do you give to what makes you most happy in your life? How much time, how much focus? Bring what makes you most happy and deeply fulfilled into your life now on a daily basis. Even a few minutes a day to start will make a big difference.

3. Say what you mean, and ask for what you need.
What is it you need to say that you haven't said? Whom do you have to say it to? What is it you truly want from others? Are you willing to ask

for it? Are you willing to accept either a yes or no in response? This is important. Give the other person the right to say yes or no. Don't take it as a reflection of you.

Speak up, express what is true for you. Do it in a kind manner. This does not mean blaming, hating, or attacking others. It simply means taking responsibility for what you feel, need, and have to express, and doing so responsibly, with dignity and certainty.

4. Take your own side now.

Are you willing to stand up for yourself? Do you take your own side, know, relish, and validate your own experiences? Spend time alone with yourself each day. Find out what's going on inside. Keep a journal, take long walks, go to the beach, hang out in the park, sit on a cushion quietly without moving, and breathe. Taste each breath fully. Become your own best friend.

5. Say no.

What is it that you need to say no to in your life that you've been going along with? Take a good look, and then, one by one, say no to it. Do it one item at a time. See how you feel then. Don't do it with anger or resentment, just do it because it's your birthright to say no to what is wrong for you. There's no other way to find and live from your authentic Self.

6. Say yes.

What is that you can say a true, wholehearted yes to, with no withholding, doubt, or hesitation? Make a list. Become aware of this. And then, one item at a time, say yes, yes, yes. See how wonderful that feels to fully accept and affirm, to give of yourself totally with a complete yes. Who in your life can you say yes to? Call them up right now and say it.

The more you keep saying no to that which is wrong for you, the more you'll be able to say yes. Your list will grow by leaps and bounds as fear and wavering depart.

7. Choose life, choose strength.

Choose to do the exercises. Remember, you have the power of choice. Fear has no authority to rule you, unless you allow it to.

PRINCIPLE 2

Letting Go of Attachment and Grasping

1. Loosen your grasp.
What are you holding on to most tightly? What is it keeping from you?

Would you be willing to loosen your grasp just a little and let go? Today loosen your grasp just a little. Tomorrow loosen it a little bit more.

2. Do not separate what you like from what you dislike.
How do you separate what you like from what you dislike? What do you chase after? What do you refuse? What do you miss by this? Today turn it around. Stop chasing after what you like, stop refusing that which you do not like. Whatever happens, just look at it and say, "Is that so?"

3. When something comes, welcome it; when something leaves, let it go.
See how your grasping creates fear. Decide that all day today you will grasp at nothing. You will allow life to take its own course. When something comes, welcome it; when something leaves, let it go. Notice how different you feel as you do so. Notice how differently the world responds to you as well.

4. Stop refusing change.
Notice something that you want to stay the same always. How long have you felt that way? Has this caused the situation to stay the same? How have you responded to these changes in the past? Have you blamed yourself or another, tried to stop it from happening? Can you now just simply allow things to change as they will?

5. Let change happen on its own.
Is there something you desperately want to change in your own time and in your own way? Notice that you are placing your own needs and ideas on a person or situation. Allow whatever is to be just as it is. Stop interfering, and allow change to happen in the way that it does, in its own time and at its own rhythm.

Even if you do not allow it, change will happen in its own time and in its own rhythm anyway. What is the value of interfering? You interfere because you want something to make you feel secure. Nothing but freedom from fear will do that. As you stop pushing and shoving, as you stop trying to change what life presents, a great deal of fear subsides, and your sense of security will grow. Try and see.

PRINCIPLE 3
Recognizing the Voices Within

1. Know what's real and what is not.
Practice making acquaintance with reality daily. Draw your attention away from your dreams, and focus it on what is actually going on. Divide a page in half. On one side write down what is happening; on the other, what you wish would take place. Allow yourself to dwell on what is actually happening. Do it for more and more time each day.

The more you do this, the stronger your ability will grow to live in reality and put fantasies on the back burner. You may even find that you like what is actually happening, that it is empowering, and that, basically, there's nothing to be afraid of.

2. Let yourself be wrong when you're wrong.
When you are wrong, admit it quickly and allow it to be so. Realize there is absolutely nothing wrong with being wrong. Write down five ways you could be wrong in a situation. Then consciously choose one of them. Be wrong consciously. See what happens.

When your fear of being wrong subsides, your ability to see and live with truth grows exponentially.

3. Enjoy each mistake.
If you've made a mistake about something, face it and be happy that you took action and now can grow. Realize that nothing terrible happened. Find out what you've learned from the mistake. If you have to make a correction, make it quickly. Forget about guilt; it is not necessary. Just realize that you are human and move forward.

Feeling What It Is like to Allow

Stop and take notice when you are lost in fantasy. See how much time you are spending this way. Write down your most prevalent fantasies and what gets them going. Now you are becoming aware. Awareness halts these fantasies from growing, right on the spot.

This exercise is for the purpose of getting the feel of what it is like to allow. Most of us fight everything that happens. We answer back, control, try to mold life to our demands. Now we are reversing this process and learning to allow. Allow yourself to allow. The more you allow, the kinder, calmer, happier, and less frightened you will become. And the more everyone around you will thrive. Try and see.

If you are with another, just be there without any expectations. Let each moment arise as it will. Don't fill the silences; don't anticipate what the other person is going to say and jump in. Let everything happen as it does. If a feeling arises, just feel it. Don't seek or avoid anything at all. Let yourself, also, be exactly as you are. Don't demand anything from yourself or others from the time you spend .

Dialoguing with the Inner Voices

This exercise helps resolve conflict within and also helps you meet and make friends with the many aspects of yourself, the different voices that live within. In the beginning, just follow the steps, take whatever comes, and make sure to give thanks for everything. Although this may seem odd at first, it quickly becomes natural. If a part of you, or a voice, asks you for something and you agree to give it, make sure you do. Do this on a regular basis. Let the parts within know when you are coming back, and make sure you can be counted on.

Spend time each day dialoguing with the voices within. Meet them, welcome them, get to know them, and, above all, allow them to speak as they will.

First, become quiet, close your eyes, concentrate within. You can pay attention to your breathing, or just become still. Get in touch with an emotion you are feeling or something that is bothering you. Feel the emotion or situation entirely. Sense what it feels like in your mind and heart. Just sense it. Don't go into words or explanations. Your job is simply to be present with whatever goes on, to watch and listen and allow.

Now ask yourself: Who is it that is feeling this?

To your surprise, a reply will come. Replies come in all kinds of ways. Some people actually feel the presence of a voice, someone who wants to speak out. Some may see an image; others just have feelings. Simply stay aware and allow the responses to your questions to come in any way they will. The more accepting you are, the more you will discover. If no answer comes, that's fine; stay with that.

Now ask again: What it is that the feeling wishes to say to you? What is it that you need to know?

Just asking this can create all kinds of responses. Some people start to cry, others to laugh. There is a wonderful sense of being cared for and attended to. Finally, someone is there to hear what's going on in your heart. You are another person to yourself. When you are present for yourself, you feel strengthened and supported.

Do not judge the response. Whatever kind of response you get, say thank you. The minute you judge or reject what you hear, that voice or part will close up. Just allow it to say all it has to. Let it know you are grateful for whatever it has shared.

Sometimes you will have heard or discovered something, but have no idea what to do next. You don't have to know. Just hear what you hear. Then ask: Is there another part within you, another voice or source of understanding, that has something to say about this? Or ask what the next step may be.

Very often, there is another part (or parts) within that pipes up in one way or another. There are other views on the matter within, different responses to the situation; sometimes you discover sudden wisdom or new ideas.

Allow the parts involved to dialogue. Allow them to go back and forth. Ask what each one needs, what each part wants, how all can live together in the greatest harmony on this matter. Sometimes there is a deadlock; a conflict may have arisen. Ask then if there is another part of you, perhaps a wiser, older, or more experienced part, that knows how to handle this, or has something to add.

At this time, your intuitive knowing arises, offering a way to bridge gaps, create harmony, offer solutions, and generally bring peace.

It can be quite startling to do this exercise. You may discover forces and feelings within that you had no idea existed. That's fine. Be gentle with yourself afterward. Give it all time to be digested and integrated. It's good to be still and breathe a bit, or take a nice walk and honor yourself for the work you did.

Some people see the results of this exercise immediately; for others it takes a while. They suddenly then find themselves capable of new action or they resolve a conflict with which they've been struggling. After doing the exercises, these changes take place silently and often unconsciously: You've dug up the soil of your mind and planted new seeds. Give them time to sprout on their own.

PRINCIPLE 4

Finding a Safe Harbor

1. What do you need to feel safe?
Make a list of whatever it is you need to feel safe. How do you go about getting it? What happens if you can't? How do you deal with the fear you feel?

What is the true danger you feel you are up against? Do you fear loss, being insulted, made a fool of? What is the real fear here? What else could bring a sense of safety and peace of mind in this situation?

Are you willing to ask for what you need? Are you willing to express to someone else what it is that disturbs you? Try doing so today. If there is something you need from another, ask for it. If there is something that disturbs you, discuss it today in a calm way.

Stop a moment and think of three times in your life when you felt particularly sad or upset. How did you handle it? Did you express it, act on it? Did you yell, blame someone, become depressed? These kinds of responses are harmful and are the cause of your feeling unsafe.

2. Handle false expectations.
Are there some expectations that do not serve you? Which ones do you

hold on to unyieldingly? Which ones cause you to be angry with others when they are not fulfilled? Which ones cause you to be angry with yourself?

List five expectations you feel protect you. Look more deeply and see if they do.

Draw a line down a page and on one side write what actually took place. On the other side, write what you expected would happen. Compare the two. Most of us let go of what actually took place and live with our expectations. Do the opposite today. Let an unreal expectation go.

3. Rid yourself of destructive challenges.

Make note of the challenges that are destructive and constructive for you. Give up one destructive challenge today. No matter what happens this week, don't pick it up again. See how you feel. Do one challenge for the entire week. Next week try a different one.

As you begin to cleanse your life of these false challenges, a great deal of fear will be leaving as well, and you will be making room for new, healthy challenges. Write these down when they appear as well. Perhaps you'll receive a job offer for something you didn't think you could do. Perhaps a new person will come into your life. Perhaps, suddenly, you will decide to paint a painting or write a play. The false challenges cover up the deeper challenges that we might have been afraid of tending to.

Make note of what your constructive inner challenges might be whenever one comes to mind. Perhaps you wanted to go back to school? Perhaps you longed for a new job or wanted to run a marathon? Perhaps you wanted to ask someone on a date or learn ballroom dancing? Don't be afraid to take note of these challenges. Once your addiction to suffering eases, once you let go of destructive patterns, there will be energy, strength, time, and ability to undertake some constructive challenge for you.

4. Let go of fighting whatever it is you are afraid of.

Spend a little time imagining yourself face-to-face with whatever it is you are afraid of.

Just imagine it. Stop fighting it, stop struggling against it. Just be there with it. Let it be any way it likes. Keep breathing. Do this until the fear of the situation starts to fade away. It will. When you stop fighting it, struggling against it, and hating it, it loses its steam and starts to dissolve.

5. Reject negative suggestions.
All day long, people are making negative suggestions to you. Consciously or unconsciously they are filling you with fear and dread. Say no to this. Do not take their suggestions in. Immediately recognize that these are just more negative expectations, designed to create fear and make you weak and susceptible to control. You have the power to refuse these suggestions (and individuals), and it is up to you to do so daily.

6. Invite all that is good and beneficial into your life.
You may find it difficult to imagine that you have the power to invite all that is good into your life. You may be surrounded by negative people, thoughts, and circumstances, but you do not have to allow them to take over. You can specifically take time and invite all that is good and beneficial into your life. Do this in any way that feels right for you. Go under a tree and issue the invitation, write it down, speak it, sing it, make a declaration, and paste it on your wall.

Some people don't feel they deserve to have anything that is good and beneficial. But this is simply not the case: You can call goodness to yourself. and you deeply deserve it. The more you have what is good and beneficial in your life, the more you can also uplift others.

7. Spend time alone each day.
You may fear being alone without noise and chatter, convinced that safety lies in the presence of good friends. Yet in fact the more you are able to be with yourself, to spend time knowing who you are, the more your inner strength and wisdom become revealed. There is a tremendous gift to be received by not making demands of yourself, just being who you are.

As you become accustomed to this, not only will you find the road to your own safe harbor, but the fear of loneliness will leave you, as you discover the power of being alone.

PRINCIPLE 5

Blessing Others: Deeds of Love

Forgiveness starts with a willingness to forgive—both others and yourself. Forgiveness is a process that needs to be done regularly, like brushing your teeth and taking a shower. Just saying, "I forgive you" is one step. It may not be enough. To really root out the depth of your anger or resentment, this forgiveness workout is wonderful. As you do the steps regularly, it becomes impossible to stay angry. After doing it one day, a certain amount of anger may be released. If more arises, it doesn't mean you haven't succeeded; it just means there's another layer there still. Keep doing the workout until you feel totally clear and loving.

1. Turn hatred into goodwill.

Think for a moment of people you do not like or respect. What thoughts do you think about them? How do they respond? Now become aware of the negative thoughts you think about yourself. What is this doing to you?

Focus on the effect your lack of forgiveness is having on you. How often do you think of the person? How much energy are you giving? How is your lack of forgiveness blocking you in other ways?

Ask yourself if you are willing to release your hatred, get it out of your life. If you are not, stop for a moment and become aware of the toll it takes on you. Has it hurt the person you are angry at as much as it has hurt you?

In order to be willing to be free of anger, do not justify the hatred in any way. See it as a poison. When it arises, simply experience the feeling for what it is, an unpleasant emotion. Do not repress or deny the energy, just experience it fully and then let it go. Say good-bye to it, see it drifting away. The ability to stay steady and centered during the experience of hatred, not to lash out, is a mark of a mature person.

ANOTHER WAY to dissolve hatred is to remind yourself that what you give to the other person, you simultaneously receive in return. If you give anger, you will receive anger. If you offer compassion and forgiveness, you will receive it simultaneously.

FORGET THE STORY THAT KEEPS THE ANGER ALIVE. Much of your anger and hatred is kept going by the story you tell yourself (and others) about it. Do not focus on the story you are telling yourself or the reasons to keep the hatred going. This story is just something you've made up. If you make up another story, if you dream up different interpretations for what happened, the hatred won't be there. In fact, you might even experience compassion or love.

FIND WAYS IN WHICH YOU ARE SIMILAR. When someone you are suspicious of, or feel afraid of, comes into your life, stop immediately; find something you like about the person, find ways in which you are similar, ways in which you could lend a helping hand. Break into your projections. Ask questions. Listen to what they tell you. Find out who the person truly is, what's important to him.

Remember all the person has done for you. When you're in the grip of hatred, it is easy to forget the larger picture in the relationship, all that has gone on. Now consciously bring to mind all the ways in which this person has benefited you. Remember his kindnesses to you. Think of qualities he has that you respect.

Also remember times in which you may have behaved the same way he did. Can you now forgive yourself for this as well as forgiving him?

If you think the person deserves your hatred, stop a moment and become aware that he may be confused about how to find happiness, and that his negative behavior is a reflection of him, not you. It is not personal, but an expression of his own unhappiness. No one who knows himself and who is fulfilled is harmful to others. See the person as someone in pain lashing out, calling for help.

How about you?

Make a list of anything this individual may have done to earn your respect at any time. Could it be that you're jealous of him? How many of these actions are in your life? If there aren't too many, choose to do some of these actions right now.

Make another list of what he's done that you disrespect. Now, once again, compare this with your own life. See if you indulge in these actions as well. If so, determine right now to eliminate them.

Take a deep breath. Don't create guilt or make all this into a pressure. Take it as a fascinating adventure. Realize that this is a potent exercise in releasing fear, self-hatred, hatred of others, and of learning to live a life based on self-respect.

FORGIVE YOURSELF. If you cannot forgive yourself for something, ask yourself what you need to do to be able to wipe the slate clean, forgive yourself, and start again. If you truly ask, eventually you will realize what is needed for reconciliation. Then do it. If you cannot do it with the person you have offended, do it with someone else. You do not need the forgiveness of another person to forgive yourself. You simply need to know what you need to feel all right about the situation now. Once you can forgive yourself, it is so much easier to forgive others as well.

Forgiveness and extending love are two sides of the same coin. The ancient exercise below is another means of offering forgiveness to others and to yourself.

2. Consciously extend love.
There is a beautiful practice in Tibetan Buddhism called Tonglen. One part of it is: Whenever you are upset with anyone (including yourself), simply send love. Even if you don't feel love, say, "I send love and light to you." It is the intention that matters, not what you happen to feel. Just keep sending love and light, no matter how you feel. Send this to yourself as well, and to any negative situation you are confronted with.

This is an amazing practice. It produces a real effect. The people to whom you are sending love and light feel it on some level. They often begin to respond differently. You also feel it. Just doing this in a focused, intentional way dissolves your own hatred and hurt.

This is such a simple exercise and yet so powerful. Some people resist doing it. They are holding on to their upset and hate. If that happens to you, simply send love and light to your resistance, and send love and light to your hatred. If you prefer your hatred, you can always stop. But why not relent for a little while and give this a try?

PRINCIPLE 6

Letting Go of Control and Domination
Much of our craving to control stems from early relationships with authority figures. As you take a new look at these individuals, take them

off their pedestals, not only do you regain your own power, but you begin the process of letting go of the need to control.

1. Make peace with your authority figures.

Who were the main authority figures in your life? What effect did they have on you?

When was the main authority figure in your life wrong? Did you allow yourself to acknowledge that? Did you allow yourself to see the truth of who he was? Can you do it now? Are you still fighting this person many years later in your life?

Take a look at this authority. List his faults and good points. What is it he needed from you? What did you need from him? What do you need from him today? Are you willing to see him as equal now, simply another individual on this earth who has a right to his views, just as you have a right to yours? What value could it be to you to make friends with this individual and take the power you have placed on him back into your own life?

2. Give up the compulsion to control.

This exercise is one of the most central and powerful in the journey to fearlessness. It is very simple. Stop a moment and notice your desire to control a person, an event, a feeling, or a situation. Feel the desire completely, and then gently let it go. Just breathe it out, see it float away, thank it for serving you, or just experience your willingness to stop controlling that person, situation, feeling, or hope. Let all be as it is for that moment. As the desire to control leaves, you may want to breathe deeply, smile, laugh, or slowly unwind.

Although you may feel that letting go of the desire to control will make you more vulnerable, the opposite is true. You will feel more in control and empowered. You are now swimming with the current of life. For some it is helpful to say that they are letting God or the universe take over. Others like to see themselves opening their hearts and minds. Letting go of the wish to control can also be done physically—you can viscerally feel the craving to control and then breathe it out, release it, see it as energy leaving.

It is important to do this over and over. Whenever something comes up that you wish to control, let it go. In the beginning it takes quite a bit of focus. After a while it becomes natural. Some situations come along where it is easy and pleasant to allow the desire to control subside. In other situations or relationships, it may be more difficult. All of this takes practice. You are building new muscles, developing a different orientation toward others and toward being in the world.

The more you let go of the craving to control, the more you are dissolving unhealthy control and becoming balanced and strong. As this process continues, not only will you grow more relaxed, open, trusting, and resourceful, but you will see wonderful new opportunities and people come into your life. Unhealthy control has kept you tight, edgy, and constricted, keeping away much that is constructive. As you let the unhealthy control go, as you open your heart, nourishment cannot help but stream into your life.

PRINCIPLE 7

Discovering Your Perfect Nature: Becoming a Friend

This chapter includes many tools that dissolve conflict both within and without. When inner conflict dissolves, it affects your outer life, as well as the other way around.

1. Identify your main conflicts.

Take a moment to notice what your main conflicts are. Write them down. Notice how the conflicts within and without are two sides of the same coin.

2. Identify true needs and wants.

Often conflict arises because you are not aware of the difference between your needs and wants. You may fight for what you want—even if it's impossible to have—while overlooking what you truly need. Just sorting this out often reduces the conflict a great deal.

Stop a moment and sort out what your true needs and values are. Are you able to ask for your needs to be met? How do you do it? Can you allow your partner to say no as well as yes?

Get in touch clearly with your specific needs and wants in a situation you are presently in that is causing conflict. Ask yourself: Do all these needs have to be met in order for me to be satisfied, to put the conflict to an end? If a need seems primary, place a check mark beside it. If it is negotiable—you can either have it or not—put a star. By doing this, you are sorting out the differences. All wants do not have to be met, but true needs do. When you learn which demands and needs are appropriate and which are not, you are not only creating boundaries but developing a strong foundation for healthy resolution.

3. How do you ask for your needs to be met?

How do you ask for your needs to be met? Do you ask directly? Do you manipulate, cajole, seduce, withhold, or demand loudly? Add other ways to this list. Be honest with yourself; no one else has to see this.

Now make a list of your reactions if you are turned down. Do you pout, withdraw, get angry, or make the person pay in other ways? Can you allow your partner to say no to you and not take it as an attack? If not, your partner becomes a slave, living at your behest.

As you do this exercise, you are taking responsibility for your own part in the escalation of conflict. Often just by doing these exercises, conflict falls away on its own.

4. End the blame game.

Blame prevents you from being clear and from taking charge of the situation. It is also a wonderful way to stop taking action and to avoid doing what is needed in the present moment. Blame can become an addiction. Nothing is ever solved through blame. It is a huge distraction. Give up all blame in this conflict. Allow both parties to be both right and wrong.

5. Give up resentment.

What do you need in order to give up the resentment and feel better? Can you ask for it? Can you give it to yourself? Can you give it to another? This is a fascinating exercise. The more you do it, the freer you will be not only of resentment but also of all kinds of obstacles in your life.

6. Discard unrealistic expectations.

Become aware of your expectations of your adversaries and also of yourself. Is it possible for anyone to meet your expectations? Is it possible for anyone to meet theirs? What are the differences between what is expected and the truth of the situation? Discard expectations that are unrealistic. A huge step toward healing conflict is seeing what is real and possible, and making peace with it.

7. Allow yourself to win.

You might enjoy conflict and hold on to it because you refuse to allow yourself to win. Once you allow yourself to be successful, you do not have to escalate conflict; you can find positive solutions with much greater ease.

How do you feel when you succeed? Are you proud of your achievement, or do you feel something else? Perhaps it's hard to let yourself win.

Make a list of all the times you succeeded at work, at a relationship, or at a project that was meaningful to you. How did it make you feel? Many people are surprised at the sorrow they feel when they succeed at something. Are you able to feel satisfied with yourself? Are you willing to succeed?

What are the ways in which you do not allow yourself to succeed? When you see what is actually going on, you can stop self-destructive behavior and stop unnecessary conflict as well.

8. Allow others to win.

Are you still clinging to an I *vs.* Them mentality? Do you realize that by holding someone hostage in a conflict, it is your energy and well-being that are being drained as well?

What do you require to allow your adversary to win? List different ways in which you can win together. List different ways in which you could benefit from turning the person from a competitor into a friend.

9. Make friends with adversaries.

Whom do you consider to be competitors? How do you feel about them? List some the times that competition made you stronger, and you both ended up friends. Can you view competition constructively? Can you see adversaries as friends, recognizing their own needs and wants, which are just as important to them as yours are to you? Can you give them some of what they want? What's the real cost to you? Wish the best for both of you. When you do, you both will win.

10. Handle predators.

Who are the predators in your life? Are they really predators—do they really wish you ill? Be sure. Spend time really looking at the full picture and make sure the relationship with the so-called predator cannot be redeemed. If it can, try to do it. If not, be clear what you're up against and take appropriate action.

11. Undo silent killers.

Keep a daily list of your particular silent killers, the ones that suddenly drain your energy, enthusiasm, and goodwill. Once you are aware of what they are, they will lose their silent power over you. As soon as one crops up, take immediate action to preserve your inspiration. Distance yourself from the silent killers, say no to their negative message and impact; consciously do whatever makes you feel positive in the moment.

12. Never give up on a person.

How willing are you to never give up on a person? How much are you willing to go through with him or her? What is your cutoff point? What behavior can't you tolerate? Why? What makes you believe in someone in the first place? What is it that takes this belief away?

Has anyone ever been there for you through thick and thin? What did that feel like? What happened when the person decided it was enough and went away? Are you there for yourself through thick and thin? Are you willing to be?

Write down the name of one person you know you will never give up on. What is it about this person that allows you to do this? What is it about you? Little by little, can you add to this list?

Finding the Precious Jewel

1. Take time to be alone: turn within.
The first step in finding your precious jewel is to be willing to stop dashing around, madly searching for it everywhere, in everyone. This is a time to take off your shoes, put your packages down, clear a space, make it simple, and just sit down and breathe.

Sit still with your back straight, legs crossed, and eyes open and pay attention to your breathing. Let whatever thoughts come, come. Let whatever thoughts go, go. Don't get caught in them, don't judge them or fight with them, let them just drift by, as if on parade. Make friends with your breathing. Let it accompany you wherever you go.

2. Pay attention to your breathing.
Let it go as it wishes to go. Just wait to be guided, instructed, uplifted, accompanied. Let the mind of peace run the show. The mind of peace is always kind, always giving. If you are moved to thought, word, or deed that is not beneficial to all, just be still until it passes. It is simply an echo of the chaotic mind.

3. Be mindful.
Pay attention to everything, even the smallest activities, like brushing your teeth or cutting an apple. No one activity is intrinsically more important than another; when we offer full mindfulness, every activity becomes electric.

4. Accept others, accept yourself.
Look around for a moment. Take note of who is around you. Really look at these people. Are you willing to accept them? What will happen if they start to accept you, too?

Make a list of the things you have trouble accepting. Can you try accepting them today? See how you feel when you do. Now make a list of the qualities you reject in others, people you would never be a friend to. Look and see if they are perhaps qualities you refuse to accept in yourself. Start to accept these in yourself right now.

Who is in your life now? Imagine yourself accepting each person;

imagine them accepting you, too. What does it feel like? If you can't imagine it with someone, why not? What has to change about this person for you to accept him or her? What has to change about you?

5. Choose life, choose love.

Love is a choice. It is not a fleeting feeling, but grows through actions and deeds of love. These are all within your power to do, no matter how you feel. A strong choice can turn everything around. These choices need to be made over and over again. Whenever something happens that is not loving, just stop and choose love. You have been given the power of choice, one of the most precious gifts of being human. Choose to choose. Choose life, choose love. Choose to be all you are meant to be. These kinds of choices open all possibilities, they move mountains. Try, and see.

We never ask the meaning of life when we're in love.

—*Bhagwan Shree Rajneesh*

MORE SIMPLE LAWS OF LOVE

- There is never a lack of love. Love is available every moment, everywhere.

- When there seems to be a lack of love, it is only that you are keeping it away.

- Love is a choice. Choose to let love into your life.

- Perception is all-important. As you perceive, so shall you live. Are you a love-finder or fault-finder?

- Be aware of the difference between real and counterfeit love.

- There are no strangers. Just friends you have not yet met.

- Self-centered thinking never brings any peace.

- Love someone totally, with no expectations.

- You don't need other people's love to fill you. You are love.

- As you give love, you learn what you are.

- Love cannot be fought for. It must be welcomed and invited.

- Don't open to get something. Just open.

- You draw to yourself whatever you feel personally worthy of.

- You will never receive from another more than you are willing to give yourself.

- There is a natural magnetism that selects for each what belongs to it.

- The real battle is an inner one and is nothing but a battle between the real and the ideal self.

- You create a mask to meet the masks of others and then wonder why you cannot love and why you feel so alone.

- Real generosity is a state of mind where one lets the other just be.

- The natural is right. The easy is right. To be yourself is right. To be yourself is all you can be. Anything else is to go astray.

How Wise Are You in Relationships?

Discover your love quotient. The higher the quotient, the better your experience in relationships, the more you can enjoy the experience, recover quickly if it ends, and be available for whatever is next. The lower the quotient, the more complications may appear.

Give yourself from 1 to 5 points for each question, with 5 the highest and 1 the lowest.

1. I usually see the best qualities of the person I am with.

2. I am open to and comfortable with many different kinds of people.

3. When I start a relationship, I do not have strong ideas about where it will go.

4. I find it easy to be pleased by the person I'm with.

5. When something starts going wrong in a relationship, I rarely start to blame.

6. When something starts going right in a relationship, I do not run away.

7. I do not escape into fantasy. The more the person seems to be the one of my dreams, the more mindful I become.

8. I require little to make me happy.

9. When a partner starts to leave, I am thankful for the time we've shared.

10. When a partner starts to leave, I do not do everything that I can to hold on.

11. It is easy for me to give freely and to receive.

12. I am not always checking on what I'm receiving, especially before I give in return.

13. It is easy for me to believe others. I am willing to give them a chance.

14. It does not take a long time for me to develop trust.

15. If I find my partner has been untruthful, I am not out of the relationship fast; I am willing and able to stay and explore why.

16. I can allow all people to be who they are, and allow myself as well.

17. I do not believe each relationship must last forever or else I've failed.

18. I know each relationship is a gift that is only given for a certain length of time.

19. I do not require constant feedback about how wonderful I am.

20. I know the Source of all love and that it never ends.

Scores

90–100 A wise one. Able to form healthy, uplifting relationships.

70–90 Doing very well. Mostly going in the right direction.

50–70 Can use more practice in relationships. Become more aware.

30–50 Tend to hide and cling. Make steady use of the exercises.

0–30 Need guidance and direction. Time to discard negative fears.

Release Anger Quickly: Easy Steps

1. Speak kindly to someone who's angry with you.

2. If someone has a complaint against you, really stop and listen.

3. Find three things you really like and respect about your opponent.

4. Give someone you are upset with the benefit of the doubt.

5. Stop trying to control the person you are angry with. Let the person be who he is.

6. If you are right in a dispute, give up being right (for that moment or day). Let the other person keep his pride.

7. If two people you know are in a fight, speak well of each one of them to the other.

8. Put the other person ahead of yourself. (You do not always need to be first.)

9. Do a forgiveness workout: Every day make a point of forgiving at least one person you haven't yet forgiven.

10. Ask yourself, *How much suffering is enough? Am I willing to feel good today?*

Remember:

You are not hurt by what people say and do. (It's your reactions that hurt you.)

Anger can become an addiction.

You can choose your responses.

The best way to defend yourself against anger is to feel good about yourself.

You cannot be insulted if you do not take it as an insult.

Being healthy and loving are more important than being right.

When you identify yourself as a victim, you attract victimizers.

When you expect something, you draw it to yourself.

You can change the whole course of your life by changing your attitude toward it.

———

May all beings have happiness and the causes of happiness.

—Buddhist prayer

———

Living on a New Basis

Love is wanting for the other what he wants for himself, even though you may not be the one able to give it to him.
—Virginia Lloyd

Living without fear does not mean never feeling fear again. At times fear is healthy and necessary. Fear teaches you not to put your hand in the fire, and to get out of the way of a runaway car. Living without fear means that fear does not take control of your life, cannot distort your thoughts and actions, and won't rule the day. You do not take actions or make decisions based upon fear; you recognize the lies it tells and can discount its false guidance. Now, when fear arises, you are able to release it—it seems simply like a shadow passing across the sun. Having done this, your energies are not crippled; you can move mountains. Above all, you have found a new basis for your life.

A life lived on a new basis is a life lived in love and goodwill. No matter how others are behaving, you can always offer love.

Consciously wish everyone well, even those with whom you have difficulties. Say to them, one at a time, "May you be peaceful, well, and fulfilled."

It doesn't take much to wish someone well. Even if you don't feel like it, do it anyway. Negative feelings need never be given the power to tell you how to behave.

No matter how you feel, just wish the person well. Then do it again. By the third time, your feelings will begin to soften. Keep on wishing that person well until you feel at ease. Remember, what you wish for others returns to you. As you wish others well, your peace of mind deepens and your life goes well.

The Gift of Peace

We cannot speak about love and peace of mind without sooner or later speaking of God, our Higher Selves, Source, Mind, or Soul. Different people describe the Source of love differently. This book is dedicated to bringing this gift to all, no matter how they define it. Whatever our individual beliefs might be, the principles of love are universal. They apply to those of all nations, races, and religions. Everyone who practices love will have the same result.

Despite many differences among us, fundamentally there is much that is the same. All of us wish to be happy and healthy, to feel loved and live fully. When these deep wishes are met, what need is there to harm others, control people, or take something away from them? It is then easy to see that the universe is filled with great abundance, and that no one need go lacking. The more we give, the more we have. It is fear that keeps this truth away.

As you deepen your own practice of love, many unexpected events, people, and miracles will appear. You will be given a chance to see for yourself how life changing and powerful just a little love can be:

> When Karen discovered that a new baby was on the way, she was thrilled and did all she could to help her three-year-old son Michael prepare for his new sibling.
>
> Although the pregnancy was normal, the delivery was difficult, and Michael's little sister was born with a serious medical condition. She was taken to the neonatal intensive care unit at St. Mary's Hospital, Knoxville, Tennessee. As the days went by, the little girl's condition worsened and the doctors told the parents to be prepared for the worst. There was very little hope.

Michael kept begging his parents to let him see his sister. "I want to sing to her," he said. His parents told him she was too sick. The second week of her life became even more difficult. Michael kept begging for a chance to sing to her, and his parents told him that children were not allowed in Intensive Care. Michael wouldn't let up, and finally Karen decided to take Michael to see his sister, whether they liked it or not. If he doesn't see her now, he may never see her alive, she thought.

Karen dressed Michael in an oversized scrub suit and marched him off into the ICU. He looked like a walking laundry basket, but the head nurse recognized that he was a child and bellowed, "Get that kid out of here now!"

Karen, usually mild-mannered, became fierce and yelled, "No. He's not leaving until he sings to his sister." Then she pulled him over to his sister's bedside.

Michael gazed at the tiny infant, tied to tubes, losing her battle to live. Then he began to sing, in the pure-hearted voice of a three-year-old, "You are my sunshine, my only sunshine, you make me happy when skies are gray . . ."

Instantly the baby girl responded. Her pulse rate became calm and steady.

"Keep on singing, Michael," his mother pleaded.

"You never know, dear, how much I love you. Please don't take my sunshine away."

The ragged, strained breathing became as smooth as a kitten's purr. Michael's little sister relaxed as healing rest swept over her.

Karen glowed, and tears fell down the face of the bossy head nurse, as all those in the ICU gathered around to watch what was happening. The very next day, the little girl was well enough to go home.

Woman's Day magazine called it "The miracle of a brother's song." The medical staff just called it a miracle. Karen called it a miracle of God's love.

What do you call it? Whatever you call it, the important point is to cultivate this miracle of love in your very own life.

Resources

Rabbi Joseph Gelberman, interfaith rabbi, All Faiths Seminary, www.allfaithseminary.org.

Noah Lukeman, agent, www.lukeman.com.

Sue Matthews, Taylor's Foundation, www.taybandz.org. This foundation raises funds for cancer research for children.

Tony Papa, author of *Fifteen to Life*, www.15yearstolife.com.

Richard Schiffman, author of *Mother of All*, www.motherofall.org.

Brenda Shoshanna, www.becomefearless.org, www.enlightenedlivinginstitute.org

Lakeesha Walrond, founder of Total Refuge, www.totalrefuge.org; email to: walrondl@aol.com. Total Refuge offers scholarships for teenagers who have survived sexual abuse, as well as workshops and a curriculum for overcoming coping mechanisms that no longer work. It also offers a prostitute relocation program and a summer camp for teenagers who have survived sexual abuse, facilitated by women who have survived sexual abuse.

Manataka American Indian Council, www.manataka.org.

Afterhours Inspirational Stories, www.inspirationalstories.com/1/149.hmtl.

A brother's song, www.rogerknapp.com/inspire/keepsing.htm.

Bibliography

Dunnigan, Neil, *Zen Stories of the Samurai* (Global Thinking Books)

Laing, R. D., *Knots* (Vintage)

Levenson, Lester, *No Attachments, No Aversions: The Autobiography of a Master* (Lawrence Crane Enterprises)

Martin, Rafe, and Manuela Soares, editors and resellers, *One Hand Clapping: Zen Stories for All Ages* (Rizzoli International Publications)

Miller, Henry, *Wisdom of the Heart* (New Directions Publication)

Nachman, Rabbi, *Advice* (Breslov Research Institute)

Sarkett, John A., *Extraordinary Comebacks* (Sourcebooks, Inc.)

Schiffman, Richard, *Mother of All* (Blue Dove Press)

Senzaki, Nyogen, *Zen Stories* (Kessinger Publishing's Rare Reprints)

Shah, Indries, *The Pleasantries of the Incredible Mulla Nasrudin* (Penguin Books)

————, *The Way of the Sufi* (Octagon Press)

Shapiro, Rabbi Rami, *Ethics of the Sages: Pirke Avot*, (Skylight Paths Publishing)

Shoshanna, Brenda, *The Anger Diet: 30 Days to Stress Free Living* (Andrews McMeel)

————, *Jewish Dharma: Guide to the Practice of Judaism and Zen* (Perseus Books)

————, *Zen and the Art of Falling in Love* (Simon & Schuster)

Tolle, Eckhart, *Stillness Speaks* (New World Library)

Yamada, Koun, *The Gateless Gate* (Wisdom Publications)

Index